Stop Stealing Sheep

Stop Stealing Sheep

& find out how type works
Third Edition

Erik Spiekermann

ADOBE PRESS

Adobe

686.
22
SPI

Stop Stealing Sheep
& find out how type works
Third Edition
Erik Spiekermann

This Adobe Press book is
published by Peachpit,
a division of Pearson Education.

For the latest on Adobe Press books,
go to www.adobepress.com.
To report errors, please send a note to
errata@peachpit.com.

Copyright © 2014 by Erik Spiekermann

Acquisitions Editor:	Nikki Echler McDonald
Production Editor:	David Van Ness
Proofer:	Emily Wolman
Indexer:	James Minkin
Cover Design:	Erik Spiekermann

ISBN 13: 978-0-321-93428-4
ISBN 10: 0-321-93428-8

9 8 7 6 5 4 3 2

Printed and bound
in the United States of America

11–06
(11–06)
11–06

STEALING SHEEP? Letterspacing lower case? Professionals in all trades, whether they be dentists, carpenters, or nuclear scientists, communicate in languages that seem secretive and incomprehensible to outsiders; type designers and typographers are no exception. Typographic terminology sounds cryptic enough to put off anyone but the most hard-nosed typomaniac. The aim of this book is to clarify the language of typography for people who want to communicate more effectively with type.

These days people need better ways to communicate to more diverse audiences. We know from experience that what we have to say is much easier for others to understand if we put it in the right voice; type is that voice, the visible language linking writer and reader. With thousands of typefaces available, choosing the right one to express even the simplest idea is bewildering to most everyone but practiced professionals.

Familiar images are used in this book to show that typography is not an art for the chosen few, but a powerful tool for anyone who has something to say and needs to say it in print or on a screen. You will have ample opportunity to find out why there are so many typefaces, how they ought to be used, and why more of them are needed every day.

We see so much type that we sometimes stop looking. This is not necessarily a bad thing, as in the case of this sign, which tells us that we may not enter this street between eleven and six, nor between eleven and six, and certainly not between eleven and six.

This is a sidebar. As you can see by the small type, the copy here is not for the faint of heart, nor for the casual reader. All the information that might be a little heady for novices is in these narrow columns; it is, however, right at hand when one becomes infected by one's first attacks of typomania.

For those who already know something about type and typography and who simply want to check some facts, read some gossip, and shake their heads at my opinionated comments, this is the space to watch.

In 1936, Frederic Goudy was in New York City to receive an award for excellence in type design. Upon accepting a certificate, he took one look at it and declared that "Anyone who would letterspace black letter would steal sheep." Goudy actually used another expression, one unfit for print. This was an uncomfortable moment for the man sitting in the audience who had hand lettered the award certificate. Mr. Goudy later apologized profusely, claiming that he said that about everything.

You might have noticed that my book cover reads "lower case," while here it reads "black letter"– two very different things. Lower case letters, as opposed to CAPITAL LETTERS, are what you are now reading; blacf letter isn't seen very often and looks life tⱨis.

I'm not sure how "black letter" in this anecdote got changed to "lower case," but I've always known it to be the latter; whichever way, it makes infinite sense. By the time you finish this book I hope you will understand and be amused by Mr. Goudy's pronouncement.

See the changes made to the sign in the last two decades: the small picture on the right is from this book's first edition, printed in 1992; the one on its left is from the second edition in 2003.

PAUL WATZLAWICK

One cannot *not* communicate.

Paul Watzlawick
(1921–2007) is author
of *Pragmatics of
Human Communication*,
a book about the
influence of media
on peoples' behavior.
"One cannot not
communicate" is
known as Watzlawick's
First Axiom of
Communication.

CHAPTER 1

Type is
everywhere.

HAVE YOU EVER BEEN to Japan? A friend who went there recently reported that he had never felt so lost in his life. Why? Because he could not read anything: not road signs, not price tags, not instructions of any kind. It made him feel stupid, he said. It also made him realize how much we all depend on written communication.

Works in most languages, avoiding tasteless mistakes: S for Salt and P for Pepper.

Picture yourself in a world without type. True, you could do without some of the ubiquitous advertising messages, but you wouldn't even know what the packages on your breakfast table contained. Sure enough, there are pictures on them – grazing cows on a paper carton suggest that milk is inside, and cereal packaging has appetizing images to make you hungry. But pick up salt or pepper, and what do you look for? S and P!

Try to find your way around without type and you'll be as lost as most of us would be in Japan, where there is plenty of type to read, but only for those who have learned to read the right sort of characters.

You've hardly got your eyes open when you have to digest your first bite of type. How else would you know how much calcium fits on your spoon?

THE WALL STREET JOURNAL.

EUROPE EDITION VOL. XXXI NO. 87

DIE ZEIT

DEUTSCHLAND 4,50 €

Womit können Sie rechnen!

WOCHENZEITUNG FÜR POLITIK WIRTSCHAFT WISSEN UND KULTUR

Frankfurter Allgemeine

ZEITUNG FÜR DEUTSCHLAND

FINANCIAL TIMES

VIRTUAL GAMES
**THE REAL WORLD
AS INSPIRATION**
PAGE 15 | BUSINESS WITH REUTERS

SUZY MENKES
**A SAVIOR FOR
A ROMAN ICON**
PAGE 7 | STYLE

VENICE BIE
SHOWING
ART THAN
PAGE 10 | CULTURE

International Herald Tribu

AY, JUNE 4, 2013   THE GLOBAL EDITION OF THE NEW YORK TIMES   GLOBAL.N

mardi 4 juin 2013 | LE FIGARO · N° 21 409 · Cahier N° 2 · Ne peut être vendu séparément · www.lefigaro.fr

LE FIGARO
économie

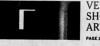

lefigaro.fr/economie

Le Monde

MARSEILLE
OUVRE SON
MUCEM
SUPPLÉMENT
4 PAGES

LA PERCÉE FOUDROYANTE
D'ASK EN AUPRÈS DES ADOS

Rubens, prince d'Europe,

WIKILEAKS L'INFORMATEUR

Breakfast for some people wouldn't be the same without the morning paper. And here it is again: inevitable type. Most people call it "print" and don't pay too much attention to typographic subtleties. You've probably never compared the small text typefaces in different newspapers, but you do know that some newspapers are easier to read than others. It might be because they have larger type, better pictures, and lots of headings to guide you through the stories. Regardless, all these differences are conveyed by type. In fact, a newspaper gets its look, its personality, from the typefaces used and the way in which they are arranged on the page. We easily recognize our favorite newspapers on the newsstand, even if we see only the edge of a page, just as we recognize our friends by seeing only their hands or their hair. And just as people look different across the world, so do the newspapers in different countries. What looks totally unacceptable to a North American reader will please the French reader at breakfast, while an Italian might find a German daily paper too monotonous.

Type says much more about a news-paper than just the information it carries.

Of course, it's not only type or layout that distinguishes newspapers, it is also the combination of words. Some languages have lots of accents, like French; some have very long words, like Dutch or Finnish; and some use extremely short words, as in a British tabloid. Not every typeface is suited for every language, which also explains why certain type styles are popular in certain countries, but not necessarily anywhere else.

What appears frightfully complex and incomprehensible to people who can read only the Latin alphabet brings news to the majority of the world's population. Chinese and Arabic are spoken by more than half the people on this planet.

áåæäàœöøçß¡¿

Some of the accents, special signs, and characters seen in languages other than English, giving each of them its unique appearance.

Newspaper design changes very slowly: the black and white picture on the right is from this book's first edition, printed in 1992; the color one on its left is from the second edition in 2003.

USA TODAY™
09.03.13
A GANNETT COMPANY

The man behind Serena
How their complex relationship works 1C

ROBERT DEUTSCH, USA TODAY SPORTS

NEWSLINE

'Never too old to chase your dreams'

Diana Nyad, 64, arrives at Key West after swimming 110 miles from Cuba without a shark cage. Story, 2A

J. PAT CARTER, AP

Elite college doesn't always mean higher pay
Some graduates with 2-year technical degrees earn more in their first jobs, research shows. **4A**

A chance to make Fed history
Janet Yellen could become the first woman to lead the Federal Reserve. **1B**

Smartwatches are on the way
Sony, Samsung expected to show off devices in Berlin this week. **2B**

Remembering David Frost
How British talk show host, who died Saturday, broke down Nixon. Opinion, **8A**

Choose the right school
Find USA TODAY's 112-page guide at newsstands or at college guide.usatoday.com.

NEWS PHOTOS
QR READER
Scan with a QR reader; AT&T code scanner available at scan.mobi. Get codes for your business at att.com/mcode.

HOME DELIVERY
1-800-872-0001
USATODAYSERVICE.COM

36
0 85903 02005 4

COPYRIGHT 2013 USA TODAY, a division of Gannett Co., Inc.

USA SNAPSHOTS®

Biking to work
Percentage of residents who say bicycling is their main

Verizon's $130B deal
Finally, telecom giant to wholly own wireless unit; move reflects competition in mobile **1B**

CBS blackout over
Ends pay dispute with Time Warner Cable; programming restored in Dallas, LA, NYC **4A**

SYRIA SELL BEGINS

JEWEL SAMAD, AFP/GETTY IMAGES

"If the Congress were to reject a resolution like this after the president ... has already committed to action, the consequences would be catastrophic."
Sen. John McCain, R-Ariz.

JEWEL SAMAD, AFP/GETTY IMAGES

"Mr. President – clear the air. Be decisive, be firm about why it matters to us as a nation to get Syria right."
Sen. Lindsey Graham, R-S.C.

J. SCOTT APPLEWHITE, AP

"This provides the president time to make his case to Congress and the American people."
House Speaker John Boehner, R-Ohio

TIMOTHY D. EASLEY, AP

"The Senate will rubber stamp what (Obama) wants but I think the House will be a much closer vote. And there are a lot of questions we have to ask."
Sen. Rand Paul, R-Ky.

J. SCOTT APPLEWHITE, AP

"Authorization by Congress for action will make our country and the response in Syria stronger. ... I look forward to the debate."
House Minority Leader Nancy Pelosi, D-Calif.

EVAN VUCCI, AP

"People's representatives must be invested in what America does abroad ... (it's time) to show the world that America keeps our commitments."
President Obama

Six key players to watch in debate over authorizing military action

Susan Davis
and Aamer Madhani
USA TODAY

WASHINGTON A week ago, it seemed the question of whether to take military action against Syria rested solely on the shoulders of President Obama.

But he has turned to Congress to authorize military airstrikes against Syria for using chemical weapons, setting up the most consequential foreign policy vote since the 2002 authorization of the Iraq War.

Obama and his supporters on Capitol Hill will have to overcome broad skepticism about the merits of military strikes and navigate the political divisions that have left Congress largely paralyzed.

The vote also cast a spotlight on key lawmakers who will be critical in determining whether or not Congress authorizes Obama to use military force. Congress is still on recess, but the arm-twisting has begun and the Syria resolution will be the first order of business in both the House and Senate when they return Sept. 9.

The debate will pit Obama and House Democratic leader Nancy Pelosi against both Republicans and Democrats skeptical of foreign military intervention. The White House will need support from Republican leaders such as Speaker John Boehner, R-Ohio, and Sen. John McCain,

▶ STORY CONTINUES ON 2A

McCain, Graham express optimism on Obama's plan

Paul Singer and Aamer Madhani
USA TODAY

President Obama's bid to get congressional support to use military force in Syria received a boost Monday as Republican Sens. John McCain and Lindsey Graham said they have more confidence the White House is developing a strategy for dealing with Syria.

McCain and Graham are key votes Obama will need to win Senate approval for the United States to launch missile strikes against Syria in response to an Aug. 21 chemical weapons attack that killed more than 1,400 people.

Obama said Saturday that he had concluded the United States should launch a strike in response to the attack, but he said he wants approval first from Congress.

McCain of Arizona and Graham of South Carolina have jointly expressed concerns that a military strike should be part of a broader strategy in Syria, not simply a random attack to punish the regime.

After meeting with Obama on Monday, they both said they believed the White House is developing a strategy that would weaken the regime of President Bashar Assad and boost Syrian opposition forces – though they said Obama has more work to do to explain this plan.

"We still have significant concerns," McCain said, "but we believe there is in formulation a strategy to upgrade the capabilities of the Free Syrian Army and to degrade the capabilities of Bashar Assad. Before this meeting, we had not had that indication."

McCain repeatedly said a congressional vote rejecting the use of military force would be "catastrophic" to U.S. interests and would destroy the credibility of the nation in the eyes of both allies and adversaries.

Graham said, "If we don't get Syria right, Iran is surely going to take the signals that we don't care about their nuclear program. ... If we lost a vote in Congress dealing with the chemical weapons being used in Syria, what effect would that have on Iran and their nuclear program?"

Both senators criticized the administration for not having a clearer strategy in Syria before now.

In Syria on Monday, Assad told a journalist with the French newspaper Le Figaro that any attack risks opening a wider war in the region.

Syria has challenged the United States and France to provide proof to support allegations that Damascus

Obama may have weakened presidency
By seeking OK from Congress, he reverses precedent. **Analysis, 3A**

At 64, a swim for the record books
Woman finishes solo Cuba-to-Florida trip

William M. Welch

to everyone," tweeted former Florida congressman and MSNBC morning host Joe Scarborough.

Looking a bit dazed and puffy from her ordeal, Nyad made brief remarks

This brings us back to type and newspapers. What might look quite obvious and normal to you when you read your daily paper is the result of careful planning and applied craft. Even newspapers with pages that look messy are laid out following complex grids and strict hierarchies.

The artistry comes in offering the information in such a way that the reader doesn't get sidetracked into thinking about the fact that someone had to carefully prepare every line, paragraph, and column into structured pages.

Design – in this case, at least – has to be invisible. Typefaces used for these hardworking tasks are therefore, by definition "invisible." They have to look so normal that you don't even notice you're reading them. And this is exactly why designing type is such an unknown profession; who thinks about people who produce invisible things? Nevertheless, every walk of life is defined by, expressed with, and indeed, dependent on type and typography.

USA Today, one of the leading newspapers in the United States, is designed to a grid.

Just as the newspaper on the opposite page is laid out according to an underlying structure of some intricacy, this book is designed within its own constraints.

The page is divided into equal parts, each of which has the same proportion as the whole page, i.e., 2:3. The page is made up of 144 rectangles, each one measuring 12 by 18 millimeters, 12 rectangles across and 12 down. This makes the page 144 by 216 millimeters, or roughly 5 $21/32$ by 8 $1/2$ inches. The columns are multiples of the 12-millimeter unit. Because there has to be some distance between columns, 3 mm (or more for wider columns) have to be subtracted from these multiples of 12 to arrive at the proper column width.

The distance between lines of type (still archaically referred to as *leading* – rhymes with *heading*) is measured in multiples of 1.5 mm.

All typographic elements are positioned on this baseline grid of 1.5 mm, which is fine enough to be all but invisible to the reader, but which helps layout and production. The discipline offered by this kind of fine grid gives the same sort of coherence to a page as bricks do to a building. They are small enough to allow for all styles of architecture, while serving as the common denominator for all other proportions.

More and more people read the news not on paper, but on TV screens or computer monitors. Type and layout have to be reconsidered for these applications.

If you think that the choice of a typeface is something of little importance because nobody would know the difference anyway, you'll be surprised to hear that experts spend an enormous amount of time and effort perfecting details that are invisible to the untrained eye.

It is a bit like having been to a concert, thoroughly enjoying it, then reading in the paper the next morning that the conductor had been incompetent, the orchestra out of tune, and the piece of music not worth performing in the first place. While you had a great night out, some experts were unhappy with the performance because their standards and expectations were different than yours.

The same thing happens when you have a glass of wine. While you might be perfectly happy with whatever you're drinking, someone at the table will make a face and go on at length about why this particular bottle is too warm, how that year was a lousy one anyway, and that he just happens to have a case full of some amazing stuff at home that the uncle of a friend imports directly from France.

Does that make you a fool or does it simply say that there are varying levels of quality and satisfaction in everything we do?

Food and design: how often do we buy the typographic promise without knowing much about the product? Stereotypes abound – some colors suggest certain foods, particular typefaces suggest different flavors and qualities. Without these unwritten rules we wouldn't know what to buy or order.

JEDEM DAS SEINE

SUUM CUIQUE

Chacun à son goût

As they say in England: "Different strokes for different folks."

The kinds of food and drink known to mankind are almost limitless. No single person could be expected to know them all. One guide through this maze of taste and nourishment, of sustenance as well as gluttony, is offered by the labels on products – as long as they are packaged in containers that can carry information. Without typography we wouldn't know which contains what or what should be used which way.

Small wonder that type on food packages is often hand lettered, because standard typefaces don't seem to be able to express this vast array of tastes and promises. These days, hand lettering sometimes means using software programs, such as Adobe Illustrator, that combine design and artwork at a level unimaginable only a few decades ago. Anything a graphic designer can think of can be produced in amazing quality.

Effects that mimic hand lettering, stone carving, sewing, or etching are all easily achieved electronically.

While it might be fun to look at wine labels, chocolate boxes, or candy bars in order to stimulate one's appetite for food or fonts (depending on your preference), most of us definitely do not enjoy an equally prevalent form of printed communication: forms.

If you think about it, you'll have to admit that business forms process a lot of information that would be terribly boring to have to write fresh every time. All you do is check a box, sign your name, and you get what you ask for. Unless, of course, you're filling out your tax return, when they get what they ask for; or unless the form is so poorly written, designed, or printed (or all of the above) that you have a hard time understanding it. Given the typographic choices available, there is no excuse for producing bad business forms, illegible invoices, awkward applications, one's ridiculous receipts, or bewildering ballots. Not a day goes by without one's having to cope with printed matter of this nature. It could so easily be a more pleasant experience.

While onscreen forms offer a very reduced palette of typographic choices, they at least provide some automatic features to help with the drudgery of typing your credit card number.

The "generic" look of most business forms usually derives from technical constraints. But even when those restrictions no longer exist, the look lingers on, often confirming our prejudice against this sort of standardized communication.

Typefaces used for business communications have often been designed for a particular technology – optical character recognition, needle printers, monospaced typewriters, and other equipment.

What was once a technical constraint can today become a trend. The "nondesigned" look of OCR B, the good old honest typewriter faces, even the needle printer, and other low-resolution alphabets have all been exploited by designers to evoke certain effects.

If you want to avoid any discussion about the typefaces you're using in your letters or invoices, you can fall back onto Courier, Letter Gothic, or other monospaced fonts (see page 175), even though they are less legible and take up more space than "proper" typefaces. You could be slightly more courageous and try one of those new designs that were created specifically to address both the question of legibility and space economy, and reader expectations.

Handgloves
BASE NINE

Handgloves
LUCIDA

Handgloves
ITC OFFICINA SANS

Handgloves
VERDANA

These are some of the typefaces designed to work well on low-resolution output devices, such as simple printers and small screens.

Typefaces designed with technical constraints.

Handgloves
LETTER GOTHIC

Handgloves
COURIER

Handgloves
OCR B

Every PC user today knows what a font is, calls at least some of them by their first name (e.g. Helvetica, Verdana, and Times), and appreciates that typefaces convey different emotions. Although what we see on screen are actually little unconnected square dots that fool the naked eye into recognizing pleasant shapes, we now expect all type to look like "print."

When each egg has data stamped on it, I wonder how the type got there. Does each chicken have its own little rubber stamp? Or do all the eggs roll by a machine, which gently impresses onto that, most breakable of surfaces? And do different sorts of eggs have different types on them? Brush Script for free-range, (see page 187), Copperplate for the expensive gourmet ones from geese and Helvetica for battery eggs?

While there is a tendency to overdesign everything and push technology to do things it was never intended to do, like printing onto raw eggs, at least we can continue our typographic training even when deciding whether the food we bought is good for nourishing or not.

I don't know whether the makers of Brunello di Montalcino deliberately chose the tall type for the labels on their wine bottles, but the widely spaced figures and the robust caps possess a certain elegance. As Monotype shows with its Andale Mono (which comes free with Microsoft software), there is room for good design even within the constraints of monospaced system fonts. Bar codes and OCR numbers are inseparable, but even that generic alphabet has already inspired a whole new type. And if you must imitate the printing on eggshells, FF Atlanta has the blotchy outlines needed to do so convincingly. While the makers of dot matrix printers try to emulate real logos, the designers of real fonts deliver the tools to print your restaurant receipts.

HANDGLOVES
FF ATLANTA

Handgloves
ANDALE MONO

Handgloves
FF OCR F LIGHT

Handgloves
FF OCR F REGULAR

Handgloves
FF OCR F BOLD

Handgloves
FF DOT MATRIX TWO

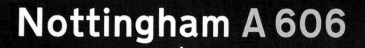

Newark	Newark
A Dark type on a light background needs some weight to be legible, but not too much.	B Light type on a dark background has to be a little thinner in order to appear as legible as the other version.

Some of the most pervasive typographical messages have never really been designed, and neither have the typefaces they are set in. Some engineer, administrator, or accountant in some government department had to decide what the signs on our roads and freeways should look like. This person probably formed a committee made up of other engineers, administrators, and accountants who in turn went to a panel of experts that would have included manufacturers of signs, road safety experts, lobbyists from automobile associations plus more engineers, administrators, and accountants.

Several countries adopted the British Transport alphabet for their road signage. Unfortunately, somebody made the type much fatter: probably an engineer who thought that more weight is more legible. The opposite is true.

You can bet there wasn't one typographer or graphic designer in the group, so the outcome shows no indication of any thought toward legibility, let alone communication or beauty. Nevertheless we're stuck with our road signs. They dominate our open spaces, forming a large part of a country's visual culture.

Traditional type for signs used to be constructed from geometric patterns so that they could be recreated by signmakers everywhere. Type as data travels more easily, so there are no more excuses for not having real type on signs.

Signage systems have to fulfill complex demands. Reversed type (e.g., white type on a blue background) looks heavier than positive type (e.g., black on yellow), and back-lit signs have a different quality than front-lit ones. Whether you have to read a sign on the move (from a car, for example), or while standing still on a well-lit platform, or in an emergency – all these situations require careful typographic treatment. In the past, these issues have been largely neglected, partly because it would have been almost impossible to implement and partly because designers chose to ignore these problems, leaving them up to other people who simply weren't aware that special typefaces could help improve the situation.

These have now been designed with a series of closely-related weights to offer just the right one, whether it's for a back-lit dark sign with white type, or for just black words on white, lit by the sun from above. The PostScript™ data generated with these types in drawing and layout applications can be used to cut letters of any size from vinyl, metal, wood, or any other material used for signs.

There are no more excuses for badly designed signs, whether on our roads or inside our buildings.

Handgloves
FRUTIGER

Handgloves
TRANSPORT

Handgloves
CLEARVIEW

Handgloves
TERN

Wittgenstein
im Kreis Wienerwald

Newark

C Too much weight makes the counters, the space inside the letters, almost disappear. Letters become blobs.

Newark

D Reversing out increases that effect. Backlit signs would look even worse (see next page).

Information

A Light type on dark shouldn't be too bold.

Information

B When lit from behind, type appears even bolder.

Information

C A thinner version of the typeface needs to be used.

Information

D Now shapes are easier to make out.

Engineers are still responsible for the signs on our roads and freeways. And they still think that Arial is the best typeface ever, simply because it is ubiquituous. But there are signs (!) of progress even in those circles: The new German DIN (*Deutsche Industrie Norm* = German Industrial Standard) committee has finally acknowledged what a lot of designers have always known: Some characters are easily confused with each other. A figure 1 looking like a lowercase l and a capital I are major offenders. The new DIN 1450 suggests a lowercase l with a loop, a capital I with serifs, and a figure 1 with a horizontal bottom stroke.

Why not use serif faces in the first place, you may ask? Interesting question, and unfortunately one not even discussed among the engineers on the committee (although there was a real type designer present). They think that serif faces are old-fashioned and could not possibly be used for signage or any other contemporary purpose.

Since this book was first published in 1993, quite a few type designers have turned their attention to this field, although neither fame nor fortune promise to be made.

The US freeways now have Clearview, a typeface designed by James Montalbano, based on the existing Highway Gothic, but actually legible and friendly. Airports the world over have adopted Frutiger, the typeface originally designed for Charles de Gaulle airport in Paris in 1976. It has recently been updated with its signage version featuring that special *l*, the *1*, and a dotted *0*.

Berlin Transit has had its special version of Frutiger Condensed, called FF Transit, since 1992. Düsseldorf Airport has signs in FF Info. Ralf Herrmann designed a typeface called Wayfinding Sans. Vialog was developed by Werner Schneider and Helmut Ness for wayfinding projects, as was Arrival by Keith Chi-hang Tam.

FRUTIGER 1450 now legible

Wayfinding Sans

FF Transit Front Positive

 FF Info Display

Arrival

Linotype Vialog

Clearview

There is less to this than meets the eye.

Glass Antiqua

Tallulah Bankhead
(1902–1968)
was a celebrated
international actress
and scandalous
public figure.
Ms. Bankhead did all
the wrong things
with consummate
flair and in the best
of taste.

CHAPTER 2

What is type?

FF Unit Light

IMPCAE
TRAIAN
MAXIMC
ADDECLA
MONSETLC

13A

EVER SINCE PEOPLE HAVE been writing things down, they have had to consider their audience before actually putting pen to paper: Letters would have to look different depending on whether they were to be read by many other people (in official documents or inscriptions), just one other person (in a letter), or only the writer (in a notebook or a diary). There would be less room for guesswork if letter shapes were made more formal as the diversity of the readership expanded.

The official Roman alphabet, as displayed in this photograph of the Trajan Column in Rome, never went out of fashion.

Below: Many digital typefaces evoke the timeless beauty of ancient inscriptions and early printing types. Adobe Trajan, designed by Carol Twombly in 1990, is a good example.

Some of the first messages to be read by a large number of people were rendered not by pens but by chisels. Large inscriptions on monuments in ancient Rome were carefully planned, with letters drawn on the stone with a brush before they were chiseled. Even if white-out had existed in those days, it would not have helped to remove mistakes made in stone. A bit of planning was also more important then, since stonemasons were sometimes more expendable than slabs of marble or granite.

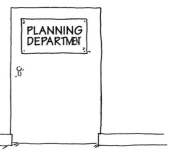

Graphic design and typography are complicated activities, but even simple projects benefit from thinking about the problem, forming a mental picture of the solution, and then carefully planning the production process.

SENATVS·POPVLVSQVE·ROMANVS

IMP·CAESARI·DIVI·NERVAE·F·NERVAE

TRAIANO·PRETTY·LEGIBLE·DACICON

MAXIMO·TRIB·POT·XVIII·IMP·VI·COS·VI·P·P

ADDECLARANDVM·VERY·SPACED·OUT

O sanctissima & Enthea Erothea matre pia, & præclaro indesinente & ualido patrocinio de gli ardenti & sancti amori, & de gli amorosi fochi, & de gli suauissimi coniugamenti infatigabile adiutrice. Si al diuino nume tuo da costei le gratie inuocate sono peruenute, Perlequale grati & accepti siano gli sui excessiui ardori & il suo gia uotato core. Rendite pietosa & arendeuola alle sue fuse oratione piene de affectuose & religiose sponsione & instante pce. Et ricordati de gli exhortatorii & diuini suasi di Neptuno al furibondo Vulcano, per te sedulamente facti, & da gli mulcibe ri laquei inuinculata cum lamoroso Marte, soluta illesamente fosti. Et alla tua superna clementia piaque cusi udirme, & præstate propitia di adimpire il determinato uoto, & socoso disio di questi dui. Il perche dal tuo cieco & aligero figliolo essendo in questa sua tenera & florida ætate apta al tuo sancto & laudabile famulato, & ad gli tui sacri ministerii disposita. da gli fredi di Diana sepata. Ad gli tui amorosi & diuini fochi (cóseruáti la natura) cú súma & ítegra diuotióe tuta si ppara. Et gia da qllo uulnerabó do figliolo l'alma sua pfossa, & fora dil casto pecto il mollicolo suo core erúcatosentétisse egli nó renuéte, ma patiéte, & másuetamte icliatose, qllo

In turn, these "official" styles of writing influenced how handwriting was looked at and how it was taught in schools or other learning centers, such as monasteries.

Page from Aldus Manutius' Hypnerotomachia Poliphili, 1499.

Today, when we are supposed to write legibly, we're instructed to "print." While we might have a hard time reading something written 200 years ago in what was then considered a very "good" hand, we have no problem reading writing from Roman times or even earlier. Likewise, the typefaces designed 500 years ago, shortly after printing with movable type was invented, still look perfectly familiar (if a little quaint) to us. We might not be using the exact same letters reproduced in the identical manner, but the basic shapes and proportions are still valid today.

For centuries, *fraktur* (literally, "broken writing") was the standard typographic style in Northern Europe. Roman typefaces were called Roman because they came from Italy and were used to set Romance languages like Italian, French, and, of course, Latin.

When communications became more international, typefaces that were more universal came into demand. Today fraktur, gothic, and similar styles are only used to evoke the feeling of a bygone era, for example, on the banner of newspapers like *The New York Times*.

They also come in handy when someone has to design a job that has Germanic undertones. The Nazis did indeed sponsor and even order (as was their way) the use of what they called "Germanic" typefaces, making it impossible for generations after World War II to use these types without historical connotations.

Some typefaces have stood the test of time and appear as contemporary today as they did 500 years ago. Their modern digitized versions have a slight edge when it comes to clean outlines.

Other typefaces were perfectly legible only a few decades ago, but can hardly be read by anybody today. It has to do with cultural perceptions, not the physical properties of the typefaces.

Far left: Aldus Manutius' first type design, printed 1499. Bembo from the Monotype Corporation, 1929, is a modern equivalent.
Left: Gutenberg's Bible from 1455.

ſl ſi ſp ſl ſt ſſ ſh ſ ct v ff

Primieramente' imparerai di fare' que=
sti dui tratti, cioe --
dali quali ſe' principiano tutte'

Prıncıpē de eodem officio.   Cornicularium.
Comentariensem. Numerarios. Adiutorem.
Abactis . A libellis . Exceptores & ceteros
officiales

Primieramente' imparerai di fare'
questi dui tratti, cioe -
dali qualiſe principiano tutte'

Principe de codem officio. Cornicularium.
Comentariensem. Numerarios. Adiutorem
Abactis. A libellis. Exceptores & ceteros
officiales

While the basic shapes of our letters haven't changed much in hundreds of years, there have been thousands of variations on the theme. People have designed alphabets from human figures, architectural elements, flowers, trees, tools, and all sorts of everyday items, to be used as initials or typographic ornaments (see right). Typefaces for reading, however, are generally derived from handwriting. Gutenberg's types followed the forms of the letters written by professional scribes in 15th-century Germany. The printers in Venice, a few decades later, also based their first types on local handwriting.

Over the centuries, cultural differences have been manifested in the way people write. Professional scribes in European courts developed elaborate formal scripts. As literacy spread, people began to care more about expressing their thoughts quickly, and less about style and legibility.

Quills, fountain pens, pencils, and felt-tip pens have all done their part to change the look of handwriting. The common denominator, the Roman alphabet, has survived all these developments remarkably intact.

Top inset: Italian manuscript, ca. 1530, shows how people wrote then. Bottom inset: From a book of writing instructions by Ludovico degli Arrighi, printed from engraved woodblocks, ca. 1521. The type on the page is Adobe Jenson Italic, designed by Robert Slimbach in 1996.

H Gill Floriated Capitals, Eric Gill
A Mythos by Min Wang and Jim Wasco

N Tagliente Initials, Judith Sutcliffe
D Rad, John Ritter

A Bickham Script, Richard Lipton

G Rosewood, Kim Buker Chansler
L Mythos

O Kigali Block, Arthur Baker
V Zebrawood, Kim Buker Chansler

E Studz, Michael Harvey
S Critter, Craig Frazier

By the same token, what was thought to be a fashionable house hundreds of years ago is still a very desirable house today. Fashion has changed remarkably since the 1400s, but people still wear shirts, trousers, socks, and shoes. The process of manufacturing them has changed, but materials such as wool, silk, and leather are still being used, and are often more desirable than their modern alternatives.

After all, the shape of the human body hasn't changed in the last 500 years, nor has the basic way we look at the world around us. Our view of things is still largely shaped by nature – plants, animals, weather, scenery. Most of what we perceive as harmonious and pleasing to the eye follows rules of proportion that are derived from nature. Our classic typefaces also conform to those rules; if they don't, we regard them as strange, at the least fashionable, and at the worst illegible.

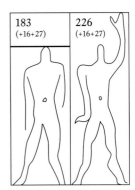

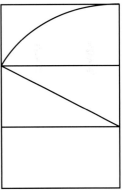

The human body hasn't changed drastically for centuries, so neither have things like shoes, fashion influences notwithstanding. Here is a collection of some footwear from the fifteenth century until today.

Some people have measured the human body to find what makes certain proportions look more beautiful than others.

Le Corbusier's Modulor (the system framing his ideas of modern functional architecture) is neatly related to a man with an outstretched arm. Not surprisingly (to anyone who's ever looked into the laws of harmonious proportions), the French architect found that the Golden Section was the underlying principle for all the measurements used in his drawings of the human body.

screen
copy

TECHNOLOGY RULES

TECHNOLOGY DESIGNS

TECHNOLOGY LEADS

First examples of a new technology rarely resemble their modern counterparts, at least not in appearance. The underlying principles, however, were there already. If they hadn't been, planes wouldn't fly, TV tubes would explode, and cars wouldn't be faster than horse-drawn carriages.

The first generation to grow up with television (those born in the 1950s) is still imitating and fantasizing about the lifestyles depicted on TV. This generation is followed by one growing up with music videos, virtual reality, and the Internet. The manipulation of sounds and images, the invention of artificial realities, and the experience of life inside man-made surroundings put to question our "natural" rules of perception. And, as with every technological and cultural development in the last 2000 years, type and typography reflect this. If current trends are anything to go by, the look of typefaces is bound to change more by the year 2023 than it has in all the years since the 15th century. The next generation of readers might consider things acceptable and, indeed, highly legible, that we today would consider ridiculous.

"It'll never catch on." Isn't that what people said about almost every major discovery or invention?

Screen fonts for phones and handheld devices brought back bitmaps, just after we had got used to "real" printing type on our printers and computer screens. At the same time, font technology enables designers to re-create every style of lettering that ever existed, from nostalgic Americana to primitive pixel type, which is now being used as a fashion statement.

From top to bottom: Zuzanna Licko's bitmap-inspired typefaces from 1987; Screenfonts for Nokia, Ericsson, and Sony; Nugget and Jackpot by House Industries; FF Peecol and F Sub Mono by Eboys.

Typefaces are **NOT intrinsically** legible

Send me a message

>Ciao, carissima

Ruf mich zurück.

Learning from Las Vegas

World Famous Buffet

Pixels are cool.
Pixels are way cool.

Sometimes a cigar is just a cigar.

Sigmund Freud
(1856–1939),
known as the father
of psychoanalysis, was
an Austrian neuro-
logist who developed
techniques of free
association of ideas
and theorized that
dreams are represen-
tative of repressed
sexual desires. Things
said without any fore-
thought sometimes
result in what is
known as a "Freudian
slip."

CHAPTER 3

Looking at type.

FF Unit Regular

HEAD

have to be big and at the top

Display

type is meant to show off the advantages **of the product inside the package it is printed on.**

TYPE IN BOOKS hasn't changed much over the last five hundred years. Then again, the process of reading hasn't changed that much either. We might have electric lights, reading glasses, and more comfortable chairs, but we still need a quiet corner, a little time on our hands, and a good story. Paperbacks crammed full of poorly spaced type with narrow page margins are a fairly new invention, born out of economic necessities, i.e., the need to make a profit. Chances are the more you pay for a book, the closer it will resemble a good historical model that dates back to the Renaissance. By the time we are adults, we have read so much that is set in what are considered "classic" typefaces that we all think Baskerville, Garamond, and Caslon are the most legible typefaces ever designed…

ADOBE CASLON REGULAR

Newspaper typography has created some of the very worst typefaces, typesetting, and page layouts known to mankind. Yet we put up with bad line breaks, huge word spaces, and ugly type, because that is what we are used to. After all, who keeps a newspaper longer than it takes to read it? And if it looked any better, would we still trust it to be objective?

SWIFT LIGHT

Small print is called small print even though it is actually only the type that is small. To overcome the physical limitations of letters being too small to be distinguishable, designers have gone to all sorts of extremes, making parts of letters larger and/or smaller, altering the space in and around them so ink doesn't blacken the insides of letters and obscure their shapes, or accentuating particular characteristics of individual letters. Another trick is to keep the letters fairly large, while at the same time making them narrower than is good for them or us so more of them will fit into the available space. Often enough, however, type is kept small deliberately, so that we have a hard time reading it – for example, in insurance claims and legal contracts.

FF META BOOK

LINES

ANYONE LOOKING AT A printed message will be influenced, within a split second of making eye contact, by everything on the page: the arrangement of various elements as well as the individual look of each one. In other words, an overall impression is created in our minds before we even read the first word. It's similar to the way we respond to a person's presence before we know anything about him or her, and then later find it difficult to revise our first impression.

We read best what we read most, even if it is badly set, badly designed, and badly printed. This is not to suggest there is a substitute for good type, great design, or clean printing, but merely a reminder of the fact that certain images are deeply ingrained in the reader's mind.

Graphic designers, typesetters, editors, printers, and other communicators are well advised to be aware of these expectations. Sometimes it may be best to go by the rules; at other times the rules need to be broken to get the point across. Good designers learn all the rules before they start breaking them.

Handgloves
FUTURA EXTRA BOLD COND.

Handgloves
ANTIQUE OLIVE BLACK

Handglov
FF ZAPATA

Handgloves
HOBO

Handgloves
ADOBE CASLON REGULAR

Handgloves
SWIFT LIGHT

Handgloves
FF META BOOK

A recurring element on these pages, as first seen on page 19, is the "Handgloves." This word contains enough relevant shapes to judge an alphabet but is a change from the industry standard "Hamburgefons." The Handgloves show off typefaces used in the sample settings or referred to in the text.

Designing typefaces for particular purposes is more widespread than most people think. There is special type for telephone books, small ads, newspapers, and Bibles, and for the exclusive use of corporations. There are also typefaces designed specially to comply with technical constraints, i.e., low-resolution printers, screen displays, monospaced typewriters, and optical character recognition. So far, all these typefaces have tried to emulate historical models. Even bitmaps have become such a model, albeit borne of necessity. Below are types that have been designed for special purposes.

Bell Centennial
designed for telephone books.

ITC Weidemann
originally designed for a new edition of the Bible.

Spartan Classified
made especially for small ads in newspapers.

Corporate ASE
Daimler Chrysler's corporate typeface.

Sassoon Primary
for teaching handwriting to school children.

1

2

3

4

5

6

43

a Cooper Black

b MESQUITE

c Arnold Böcklin

d CAMPUS

e Tekton

f Snell Roundhand

This is a typographic puzzle. Which typeface do you think fits which shoe? The answers are on the next page, but don't look now – that would be cheating. Remember which letter from the boxes on this page goes with which number from the opposite page, then turn the page and check against my personal favorites.

In some cases it is very easy to spot a typographic faux pas.

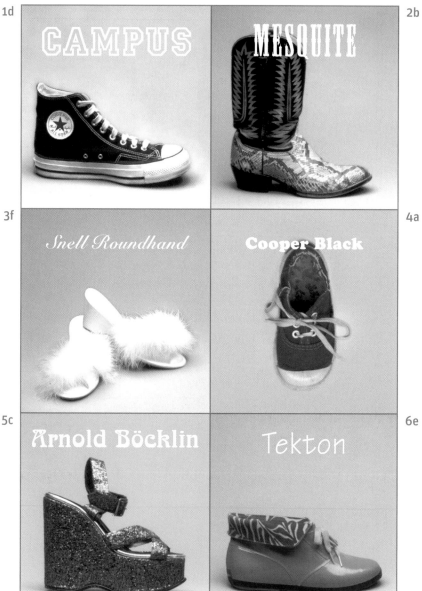

1d CAMPUS

2b MESQUITE

3f *Snell Roundhand*

4a **Cooper Black**

5c Arnold Böcklin

6e Tekton

No one would use the same shoes to go dancing, run a mile, climb the north face of the Eiger, and walk to the office – not many people, anyway. While your feet may pretty much stay in the same shape, they need different types of support, protection or, indeed, enhancement to perform all the above tasks and many more besides.

This also applies to type. Sometimes the letters have to work hard to get across straight facts or numbers, or they may need to dress up the words a little to make them seem more pleasant, more comfortable, or simply prettier.

Some shoes fit your feet better than others, and you get to like them so much that you just want to keep buying the same kind over and over. Your friends, however, might begin to give you a rough time over your taste in footwear, so why not buy a few pairs of the same model but in different colors? Now you have more choices at the same comfort level.

Where's the analogy with type? Well, you can print it in different colors, on different backgrounds, dark on light, or light on dark. It will always appear as if you are actually using more than one typeface.

Your personal choice of typefaces to match the shoes will probably be quite different from the ones shown here. With more fonts to choose from than there are shoes in your typical shoe store, the task is daunting.

Luckily, the intended typographic purpose narrows down the choice as much as where you will be wearing your shoes. Fortunately for the fashion-conscious designer, there are many options to choose from, even for similar design applications.

Cooper Black – see opposite page – is a very popular typeface, and was even more so thirty-five years ago. It has its advantages: nice and cuddly, heavy, and relatively unusual. But if you think it's been used a little too often, you can try Goudy Heavyface, ITC Souvenir Bold, Stempel Schneidler Black, or ITC Cheltenham Ultra. Compare them to each other and you will see they're all quite different, but might do the same job just as effectively.

Not all of us want to be seen wearing the same shoes as everybody else.

Handgloves
GOUDY HEAVYFACE

Handgloves
ITC SOUVENIR BOLD

Handgloves
STEMPEL SCHNEIDLER BLACK

Handgloves
ITC CHELTENHAM ULTRA

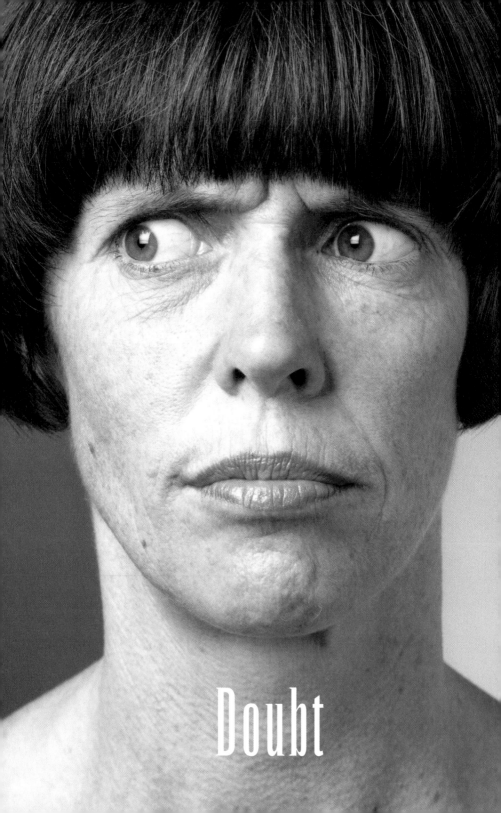

Doubt

So type has its practical uses – it can walk, run, skip, jump, climb, and dance. Can it also express emotions? Of course. If you look closely at a letter, you can see personality expressed in its physical characteristics: light or heavy, round or square, slim or squat. Letters can stand at attention next to each other like soldiers or they can dance gracefully on the line. Just as some words sound better than others, some words look nicer than others. That may be because we don't like the meaning of the word, but often we've formed an opinion before we've even read it. Isn't it nice that the *o* imitates the way we make our lips round to pronounce it? And how could the *i* stand for anything but the pointed sound it has in "pick"?

Dark emotions call for a black typeface with sharp edges; pleasant feelings are best evoked by informal, light characters. Or are they? The trouble is that as soon as you select a typeface that looks appropriate, put it on a page, surround it with space and perhaps other elements, it can take on a totally different look. So for the moment, we'll stick to choosing appropriate typefaces.

Runic Condensed is a typeface from Monotype. Released in 1935, it replicates a late nineteenth-century display type.

Bodega Sans adopts ideas from the high period of Art Deco. It was designed by Greg Thompson in 1990; its seriffed companion followed in 1992.

Block is a family of typefaces originally designed by H. Hoffmann in 1908, with many subsequent versions released through 1926. Block simplified the setting of justified display lines with a system of capital and lowercase letters of varying widths that allowed the compositor to use the more extended alternate characters to fill out short lines. Block was the staple jobbing font for German printers well into the 1960s, when phototypesetting replaced hot metal. The irregular "mealy" outlines appeal to a modern audience, who like that recycled, used-before look.

Neville Brody designed the movie titles for *A Rage in Harlem*. In 1996, he was persuaded to turn that design into a full family of typefaces. The informal weight has an unusual name: Harlem Slang.

In 1937, Morris Fuller Benton designed Empire for *Vogue* magazine. David Berlow revived it in 1989, adding an italic and a lowercase, both unavailable in the original.

Runic Condensed is slightly awkward and definitely not suited for long passages. Its spiky serifs and exaggerated letterforms do not agree with classic ideas of beauty and fine proportion. If unusual letterforms express uneasy feelings, these other condensed types might be a good choice.

RUNIC CONDENSED

BODEGA SANS LIGHT

BLOCK EXTRA CONDENSED

BODEGA SERIF LIGHT

HARLEM SLANG

BUREAU EMPIRE

Surprise

Some words are much more fun to find an appropriate typographic equivalent for than others. (Surprise, surprise.) It may be fairly difficult to find a majority agreement on the right typeface to spell "doubt," but this one shouldn't cause any problems. What's more unexpected, more surprising, than someone's handwriting? The best casual typefaces have always managed to carry some of the spontaneity of handwritten letters into the mechanical restrictions of typesetting. Even the names of some typefaces make you want to choose them. How about this one: Mistral – a cool wind blowing from the north into southern France. And indeed, in the south of France it seems to have become the standard typeface for every shopfront and delivery van. In case you don't agree that Mistral suggests surprise, here are some alternatives.

Mistral was designed by Roger Excoffon in 1955. His other typefaces – Antique Olive, Choc, Banco – also show a characteristic Gallic style and have been enormously successful in France and other European countries. Susanna Dulkinys took Letter Gothic and replaced some characters with others that have similar shapes, but different meaning. The *S* is a dollar sign; the *p* is the Thorn – used in Icelandic, Old English, and phonetics; the *i* is an upside-down exclamation mark as used in Spanish for quotes; and the *e* is the Euro currency sign.

The complete freedom offered by computer applications makes type even more flexible – if a word doesn't look right when first set, you can manipulate the outlines until it does exactly what you want.

"Surprise" is shown at right in its unaltered form. We didn't like the join between *S* and *u,* so we created outlines in Adobe Illustrator, cleaned up that detail (and a few others), and placed it in our photograph, where you can see the revised word. Most people would believe that it had been written by someone with a felt-tip pen, not simply set as part of a complete page.

MISTRAL

LETTER GOTHIC SLANG

DOGMA SCRIPT

FB DIZZY

OTTOMAT BOLD

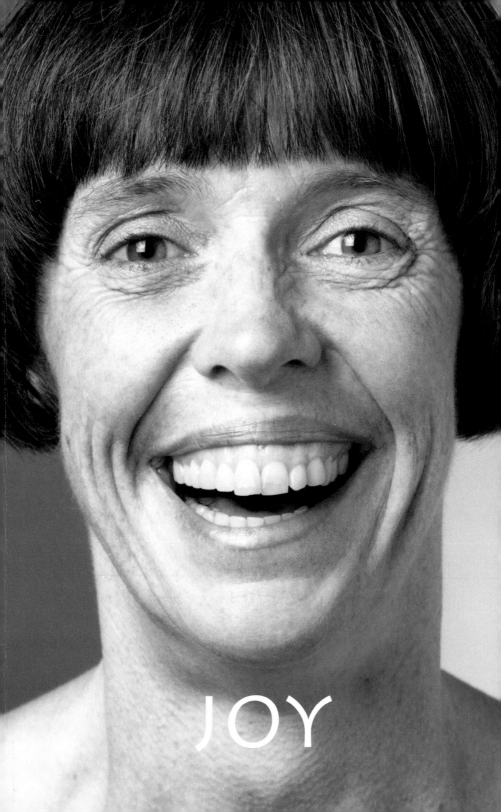

JOY

The more characters in a word, the more chances there are to find the right letterforms to express its meaning. This word doesn't give us a lot of choices, just three characters: *j o y* or *J O Y*. Seeing that the lowercase *j* and *y* look so similar, an all-capital setting will work better with this one. All three typefaces here have a generous feel to them – open forms with confident strokes and a sense of movement.

ITC Kabel, Syntax, and Lithos are modern interpretations of classical letterforms; they maintain a chiseled look without formal stroke endings, which are known as serifs.

The letter Y, a latecomer to the Latin alphabet, is called *i grec* in French (Greek *i*). Its shape is derived from one of the calligraphic variations of the Greek upsilon.

The original Kabel, designed by Rudolf Koch in 1927, has distinct Art Deco overtones, whereas International Typeface Corporation's 1976 version has a very generous x-height and is more regular and less quirky.

Syntax has the proportions of ancient Roman letters, but no serifs, making it both contemporary and classic looking. It was designed by Hans-Eduard Meier in 1968.

Lithos is Carol Twombly's 1989 rendering of Greek inscriptions – just as elegant as Roman capitals, but less restrained. This face became an instant success and graphic designers have been using it for all sorts of trendy purposes, which goes to show that a classic can also be cheerful and modern.

KABEL BOOK

ITC KABEL BOOK

SYNTAX

LITHOS REGULAR

It is nice to see that some words carry their own explanation in the letters. These free and easy shapes certainly make you think of a joyful person with arms in the air.

Handgloves
KABEL BOOK

Handgloves
ITC KABEL BOOK

Handgloves
SYNTAX

HANDGLOV
LITHOS REGULAR

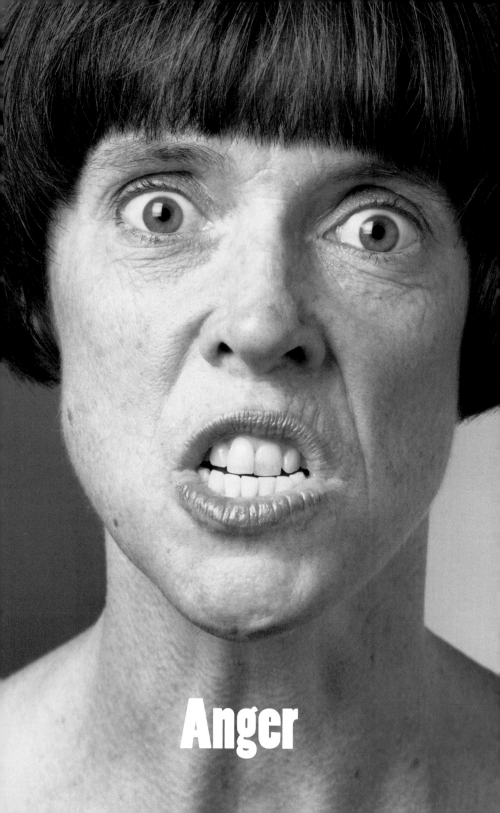

Anger

Anger, like doubt, can be described as a dark feeling that calls for a black, heavy typeface. Anger is not as narrow as doubt. It needs room to expand, sometimes to shout out loud. It helps if the letters are not perfectly worked out and closed in on themselves, but rather a little irregular, leaving room for our imagination. A well-balanced Univers or Helvetica would not do.

Most really black typefaces have been overused because there aren't enough choices for the designers of posters and tabloid newspapers. These kinds of faces can be set with hardly any space between letters, which makes a large impact in a small space.

Futura Extra Bold and ITC Franklin Gothic Heavy have been favorites for a long time. Inspiration for Solex – designed by Zuzana Licko in 2000 – reportedly came from two principal sources: Alternate Gothic and Bauer Topic (also known as Steile Futura) and is her exploration of the industrial sans serif genre. Eagle is FontBureau's 1989 adaptation of Morris Fuller Benton's famous titling, Eagle Bold, drawn – caps only – in 1933 for the National Recovery Administration. Officina Black adds weight to my sans and serif family, which was first published by ITC in 1990. The new versions were digitized by Ole Schäfer. Giza brings back the glory of the Victorian era. David Berlow based the family (1994) on showings in Figgins' specimen of 1845.

And all the way from the 1960s, Roger Excoffon's Antique Olive Nord shows that good typefaces are indestructible.

Flyer Extra Black Condensed, designed in 1962 by Konrad Bauer and Walter Baum. Poplar is a 1990 revival from Adobe of an old wood type from the mid-nineteenth century. Block Heavy (1908) is the fattest member of the family. Its outlines are deliberately irregular, which helped prevent damage when metal type was printed on heavy platen presses. You could call it a pre-stressed design.

Angst and Franklinstein are both rightly named. Jürgen Huber and Fabian Rottke designed them – respectively – in 1997 for FontFont's Dirty Faces™ group.

Anger!
FLYER EXTRA BLACK CONDENSED

Anger!
POPLAR

Anger!
BLOCK HEAVY

Anger!
ANGST HEAVY

FRANKLINSTEIN

Handgloves
FLYER EXTRA BLACK CONDENSED

Handgloves
POPLAR

Handgloves
SOLEX BLACK

Handgloves
ITC OFFICINA BLACK

Handgloves
BLOCK HEAVY

Handgloves
FUTURA EXTRA BOLD

Handgloves
ITC FRANKLIN GOTHIC HEAVY

Handgloves
GIZA NINE THREE

Handgloves
EAGLE BLACK

Handglov
ANTIQUE OLIVE NORD

Serif

Handgloves

LYON TEXT NO. 2

Sans Serif

Handgloves

FF BAU

Script

FF MISTER K

Display

Handgloves

FANFARE

Symbols

GLYPHISH

Feelings

There are seven deadly sins, seven seas, and seventh sons of seventh sons, but thousands of typefaces. Someone had to come up with a system to classify them, since describing how different type designs express different emotions just isn't exact enough. Unfortunately, there is not only one system, but quite a few, all of them too involved for anyone but the most devoted typomaniac. So here's the most rudimentary method of classifying type. It's not historically correct, nor does it give a complete overview of the available choice of fonts. It simply shows that with just a few basic principles, hundreds of ways of designing typefaces become possible, the same way a few basic emotions evoke a million ways to make a face.

The unofficial type classification – do not confuse with the official one on this page.

In case anyone wants it on record: here's the official Adobe type classification. We have chosen a typical typeface for each category, trying to avoid all the best-known ones.

Venetian

Handgloves
CENTAUR

Garalde

Handgloves
SABON

Transitional

Handgloves
JANSON TEXT

Didone

Handgloves
ITC BODONI

Slab Serif

Handgloves
MEMPHIS

Sans Serif

Handgloves
SYNTAX

Glyphic

Handgloves
FRIZ QUADRATA

Script

Handgloves
POETICA CHANCERY

Display

HANDGLOVES
PENUMBRA MM

Blackletter

Handgloves
WILHELM KLINGSPOR GOTISCH

Non-Latin

却枂儔兇剹泮
ADOBE MING

Altitudines membrorum Virilium.

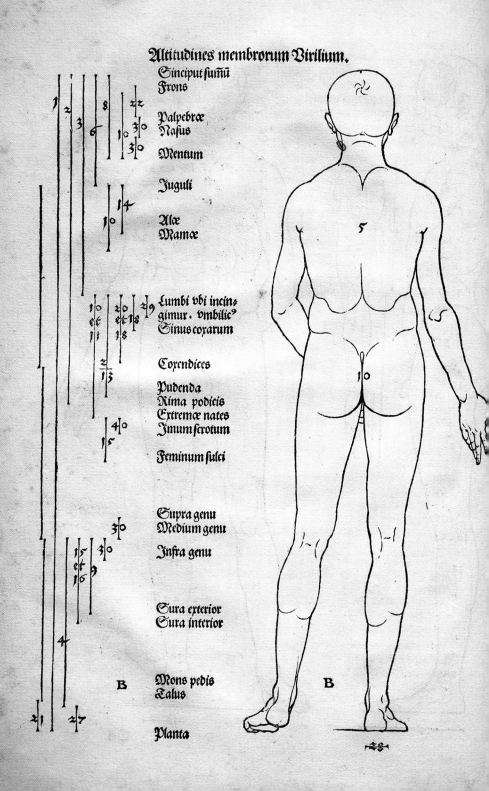

Sinciput summū
Frons

Palpebræ
Nasus

Mentum

Juguli

Alæ
Mamæ

Lumbi vbi incin-
gimur. vmbilic°
Sinus coxarum

Coxendices

Pudenda
Rima podicis
Extremæ nates
Imum scrotum

Feminum sulci

Supra genu
Medium genu

Infra genu

Sura exterior
Sura interior

B   Mons pedis
Talus

Planta

B

Scientists have not been content with just calling the human face "beautiful" if it meets certain ideals, or "ugly" if it doesn't. They have had to go out and measure proportions of nose to jaw, forehead to chin, and so on, to establish why some faces are more appealing than others. Typographers and graphic designers often choose typefaces for the very same reason they might fancy a person: They just like that person. For more scientifically minded people, however, there are specific measurements, components, details, and proportions describing various parts of a letter. While these won't tell you what makes a typeface good, they will at least give you the right words to use when you discuss the benefits of a particular face over another. You can say "I hate the x-height on Such-a-Gothic" or "These descenders just don't work for me" or "Please, may I see something with a smaller cap height?" and you'll know what you are talking about.

For his book *De symmetria partium humanorum corporum,* printed in 1557, Albrecht Dürer measured every part of the human body.

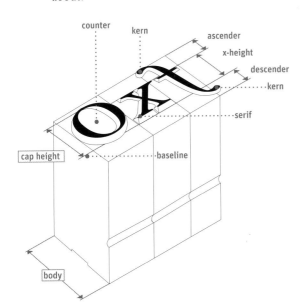

By now you will have noticed that I use the word *typeface* and *type* to describe what people these days refer to as a font. Much of the terminology used today comes from the era of metal type. The spaces between lines are still (and not very accurately) described as leading, even though they certainly aren't made up of strips of lead anymore. A font was a prescribed grouping of letters from one typeface assembled by a type foundry for sale. These were apportioned to the number of letters used most frequently in any given language. The English printer who bought a French font of type, for instance, soon noticed its lack of sufficient k and w and its large supply of q. Italian demands a larger number of c and z; Spanish, far more of d, t, and all the vowels; German, more capital letters and more z, but less y.

We design typefaces and we produce fonts. And throughout this book, I maintain that distinction. While the language of typography still adheres to some rules, there really aren't any standards for type designers to follow. Typographic features, such as large x-heights, wide counters, and exaggerated ascenders, are no less slaves to fashion than the perpetual changes in skirt lengths determined on Paris runways. The size of type, indicated in points (a point is .01384 inch; 12 points = 1 pica; 6 picas = 1 inch), is only a reminder of a historical convention, when type was cast on a body of metal. The body size of all 12-point type would have been the same, but the actual image on that body could be vastly different. Have a look at the 20-point types below – they don't have very much in common apart from the baseline.

The moral?
What you see is what you get – trust your eyes, not the scientific measurements.

Sizes Sizes **Sizes** Sizes Sizes

1 Express	40°C	Programme selection...
2 Minimum iron	40°C	Settings ⁞...
3 Automatic	40°C	
4 Woollens ⌾	30°C	12:20

START

PC ●

While metal letters could be made to any width and height, digital type has to conform to multiples of the smallest unit: the pixel. That is essentially a tiny black mark on the surface, be it screen or paper. Every character has to be a certain number of pixels wide and high. This is not a problem when the letters are made up of 600 pixels per inch (or about 24 pixels per mm), as is the case with modern laser printers. Those pixels are not discernible to our eyes, and we are happy to believe that we are seeing smooth curves instead of little squares fitted into tight grids.

On most screens, only 72 pixels make up one inch (roughly three pixels per mm). We could see each and every one of them, if engineers hadn't already found ways around that (read more on page 133). Computer screens, however, are not where we read most of our type these days. Smart phones, computers, and tablets all have high-resolution screens, but microwave ovens, espresso makers, and all the other gadgets around us all still use small and modest displays. More often than not that means black on greenish gray or green on black. And the type unmistakably consists of bitmaps, which means that an 8-point letter is actually made up of eight pixels. If we allow six pixels above the baseline, including accents, and two below for descenders, that'll leave only three or four pixels for a lowercase character. In spite of these restrictions, there are hundreds of bitmap fonts, all different from one another by only a few pixels, but enough to prove that typographic variety cannot be surpressed by technological restraints.

A dialog with a washing machine does not have to be an unpleasant experience, at least visually. Even a simple pixel font can appear friendly. Yellow type on a dark screen is also easier on the eye than green on black.

Editing pixels is like a game of chess: there are only a few black and white squares, and every move has enormous consequences.

Rather than try and imitate Times New Roman or Helvetica on a tiny chessboard, bitmap fonts have to make virtue out of necessity. It is amazing to see how much one can push the critical shape of each letter toward some almost abstract black and white graphic, and still make us think we're reading roman characters.

Joe Gillespie has designed a series of very small bitmap fonts for use on screens, appropriately named Mini 7, which is the size they are supposed to be set in. Another set of bitmap fonts for tiny sizes (only three pixels tall!) comes from Eboys, who have turned the bitmap look into an art form.

The makers of devices with small display screens would be well advised to look at these examples and in the future keep their engineers from making bitmap fonts.

HANDGLOVES
HANDGLOVES
HANDGLOVES
HANDGLOVES
HANDGLOVES
HANDGLOVES
Handgloves
Handgloves

The Mini Series, all at 7pt. In the first six lines, capital letters are five pixels tall, while the mixed words have that many pixels for a lowercase letter.

Handgloves

Handgloves

FF Xcreen uses only three pixels for a lowercase character, but as this is not a true bitmap but actually an outline font, the pixels can be scaled to any size, ranging from sublime to ridiculous.

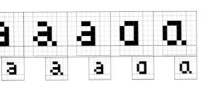

What a difference a dot makes: With only five pixels for the x-height, a type designer has to give up a lot of creative ego and be content moving one pixel at a time.

The best part about playing the piano is that you don't have to lug around a saxophone.

Berthold Akzidenz Grotesk Condensed

Gerry Mulligan
(1927–1996), master of the baritone saxophone, was one of the most versatile figures of modern jazz. He wrote his first arrangements and jazz compositions when he was still in his teens, and was part of the cool jazz scene in the 1940s; especially noteworthy were his pianoless groups in which his intricate and carefully balanced composing and arranging brought improvisation to new heights. He occasionally played the piano.

CHAPTER 4

Type with a purpose.

YOU KNOW WHAT IT'S LIKE. It's late at night, your plane leaves at 6 AM, you're still packing, and you just can't decide what to put into that suitcase.

Picking typefaces for a design job is a very similar experience. There are certain typefaces you are familiar with. You know how they will behave under certain circumstances, and you know where they are. On the other hand, there are those fashionable types that you've always wanted to use, but you're not quite sure if this job is the right one to experiment on. This is just like choosing which shoes to take on your trip – the comfortable ones are not the height of fashion, but the fashionable ones hurt. You might be able to stand them for a short reception, but not for shopping, let alone for a hike into the countryside.

Before you pack your font suitcase, you need to look at the task ahead. Strike a balance between practicality and aesthetics – that's what design is all about.

While nobody has ever classified typefaces according to their problem-solving capabilities, many typefaces we use today were originally designed for particular purposes. Some of them are mentioned on page 33, but there are many more. Times New Roman was specially produced in 1931 for the London newspaper that gave its name to the typeface. In the late 1930s, Mergenthaler Linotype in the USA (led by Chauncey H. Griffith) developed a group of five typefaces designed to be legible despite the rigors of newspaper printing. They were, not surprisingly, called the "Legibility Group," and two of them are still very popular today: Corona and Excelsior. It might seem odd that legibility has to be a special concern when designing a typeface, but there are plenty of fonts around that are meant to be seen, not read; these typefaces are very much like clothes that look great but barely protect the wearer from the elements.

Gulliver is Gerard Unger's solution for many problems in newspaper design and production. It fits 20% more copy into the columns without sacrificing legibility and is sturdy enough to be carelessly printed on recycled paper. Quite a few newspapers around the world use it to good effect.

Coranto is Unger's latest typeface for newspapers. Designed in 2000, it is being used for *The Scotsman* as well as newspapers in Sweden and Brazil.

Tobias Frere-Jones' work on Poynter was sponsored by the Poynter Institute to answer the same question. He asked himself: how to retain copy without losing readers? As we read best what we read most, the designer stuck to familiar forms and returned to Hendrik van den Keere's seventeenth-century oldstyle roman. As different methods of reproduction and printing may add or reduce weight by a fraction, Poynter Oldstyle Text is offered in four grades.

Handgloves
TIMES NEW ROMAN

Handgloves
CORONA

Handgloves
EXCELSIOR

Handgloves
GULLIVER

Handgloves
CORANTO

hand hand hand hand
POYNTER TEXT ONE   POYNTER TEXT TWO   POYNTER TEXT THREE   POYNTER TEXT FOUR

Handgloves
POYNTER OLDSTYLE BOLD

Going on vacation doesn't necessarily mean traveling to a warm climate, but it always means we can leave behind many of our conventions, including the way we normally dress — or have to dress, as the case may be. You pick your clothes according to what is practical: easy to pack, easy to clean, and according to what is fun: casual, colorful, loose, and maybe a little more daring than what you would wear in your hometown. The typographic equivalents are those typefaces that are comfortable to read, but which may be a little more idiosyncratic than your run-of-the-mill stuff. Serifs, too, can be casual, and "loose fit" is actually a type-setting term describing letters that have a comfortable amount of space between them. As it happens, quite a few of the very early typefaces from the Renaissance and their modern equivalents fit that description. They still show their kinship with Italian handwriting, which by necessity had to be more casual than rigid metal letters. If you were a scribe in the papal office and had to write hundreds of pages every day, you wouldn't be able to take the time to fuss over formal capitals. So the scribes developed a fluent, cursive hand-writing, which today we call italic, because it was invented in Italy. You will have noticed that this whole page is set in a script font, and it feels quite comfortable. A conventional rule says that you can't set whole pages, let alone books, in the italics of a typeface. The only reason it might not work is because we're not used to it. As pointed out on page 41, we read best what we read most. But that's no reason not to take a vacation from our daily habits and look at something different, at least once a year.

Some typefaces have a leisurely look about them while conforming to everyday typographic expectations. Others were born with unusual, yet casual, shapes and make the best of it.

Stempel Schneidler combines friendly letter shapes with high legibility – you can use it every day without it becoming restrictive like a necktie.

A typeface that looks casual, even "nice," but is still good for real work is ITC Flora. It was designed by the Dutch type designer Gerard Unger in 1980 and named after his daughter. Ellington, released in 1990, is a design by Michael Harvey, the English lettering artist and stone carver. Both typefaces are quite unusual and therefore not often thought of as useful text faces. But they are.

Many typefaces designed to look "friendly" tend to appear patronizing. They can be so nice that you quickly get tired of them. When you're looking for casual typefaces, the obvious candidates are, of course, the scripts. Most, however, are not suited to long spells of reading, just as sandals are very comfortable, but not when walking on rocky roads.

To make a typeface look as casually elegant as FF Fontesque takes a lot of experience and effort. Nick Shinn designed Fontesque in 1994. It wasn't his first design, and it shows. Cafeteria indeed started on Tobias Frere-Jones' napkin, and he managed to balance activity with legibility in this freeform sans serif face.

Handgloves
STEMPEL SCHNEIDLER

Handgloves
ITC FLORA

Handgloves
ELLINGTON

Handgloves
FF FONTESQUE

Handgloves
FB CAFETERIA

Most type is used for business communication of one sort or another, so it has to conform to both written and unwritten rules of the corporate world. Just as business people are expected to wear a suit (plus, naturally, a shirt and tie), text set for business has to look fairly serious and go about its purpose in an inconspicuous, well-organized way. Typefaces, such as Times New Roman and Helvetica fit this bill perfectly, not by their particular suitability but more by their lack of individualism.

However, just as it is now permissible in traditional business circles to wear fashionable ties and to even venture into the realm of Italian suits that are not black or dark blue, typographic tastes in those circles has widened to include other typefaces, from Palatino to Frutiger.

Generally, it is very simple to classify a particular business by the typefaces it prefers: the more technical a profession, the cooler and more rigid its typefaces (Univers for architects); the more traditional a trade, the more classical its typefaces (Bodoni for bankers).

The trouble is that there is no law against speculators employing a true classic, trustworthy typeface in their brochures, lending these unsavory entities typographic credibility, although nothing else.

To show the subtle differences between fonts at this size, we've set the copy at left in a variety of types, one for each paragraph. Handgloves at the bottom of this column shows them in sequence.

Frutiger, originally designed in 1976 by Adrian Frutiger for the signage at the Charles de Gaulle airport in Paris, has become one of the most popular typefaces for corporate use.

Palatino, designed by Hermann Zapf in 1952, owes its popularity – especially in the USA – largely to its availability as a core font on PostScript laser printers. It is nevertheless a welcome alternative to other, less suitable, serif fonts.

Adrian Frutiger designed Univers in 1957. It was the first typeface to be planned with a coordinated range of weights and widths, comprising twenty-one related designs, recently expanded to 59 weights (see page 89).

ITC Bodoni is one of many redesigns of Giambattista Bodoni's classic typefaces from the late eighteenth century. It shows more color and stroke variations than other Bodoni revivals, and is available in three versions for different sizes.

Handgloves
FRUTIGER

Handgloves
ITC BODONI SIX

Handgloves
PALATINO

Handgloves
ITC BODONI TWELVE

Handgloves
UNIVERS

Handgloves
ITC BODONI SEVENTYTWO

FF UNIT MEDIUM

If it were just a little heavier, News Gothic by Morris Fuller Benton, 1908, would be a favorite workhorse typeface. ITC Franklin Gothic, a 1980's re-design of Benton's original typeface from 1904, has more weights as well as a condensed and a compressed version plus small caps.

Lucas de Groot designed his Thesis family from the out-set with 144 weights. The Thesis Sans family has become an alternative to Frutiger in cor-porate circles, as it is both neu-tral and versatile. Lucida Sans, by Kris Holmes and Charles Bigelow, 1985, has sturdy, rug-ged letter shapes. Its sister typeface, Lucida, remains one of the best choices for business communications printed on laser printers and fax machines.

FF Meta has been called the "Helvetica of the 90s." While that may be dubious praise, Meta is a warm, humanist alter-native to the classic sans faces. Lots of detail make it legible in small sizes and "cool" rather than neutral. You should also look at the condensed weights of Frutiger as useful, but underused alternatives.

FF Profil is one of a new gene-ration of modern sans faces. Designed by Martin Wenzel in 1999. PTL Skopex Gothic is Andrea Tinnes' take on the classic Angloamerican genre, it gives News Gothic an interesting twist.

■ Calling a typeface "a real workhorse" doesn't mean that others don't work, it just means that it is one of those that don't look very glamorous and is consequently not likely to be known by name; such types, however, are used every day by designers and typesetters because of their reliability.

● If you set a catalog for machine parts, or instructions for using a fire extinguisher, you're not worried about subtly curved serifs or classicist contrast. You need letters that are: clearly distinguishable; compact, so enough of them fit into a limited space (is there ever enough space?); and sufficiently sturdy to withstand the rigors of printing and copying. Here's what is needed in a hardworking typeface:

① A good regular weight – not so light that it will disappear on a photocopy (every-thing, it seems, gets copied at least once these days), and not so heavy that the letter shapes fill in.

② At least one bold weight, with enough contrast to be noticed, to complement the regular weight.

③ Very legible numerals – these must be particularly robust because confusing figures can be, in the worst of cases, down-right dangerous.

④ Economy – it should be narrow enough to fit large amounts of copy into the avai-lable space, but not actually compressed beyond recognition. A typeface fitting this description would also fare very well when faxed.   FF MARK BOLD

Handgloves
Handgloves
NEWS GOTHIC

Handgloves
Handgloves
ITC FRANKLIN GOTHIC

Handgloves
Handgloves
THESIS SANS

Handgloves
Handgloves
INTERSTATE

Handgloves
Handgloves
GOTHAM

Handgloves
Handgloves
FF META

Handgloves
Handgloves
FF META CONDENSED

Handgloves
Handgloves
FRUTIGER CONDENSED

Handgloves
Handgloves
FF PROFILE

Handgloves
Handgloves
PTL SKOPEX GOTHIC

Handgloves
Handgloves
ITC OFFICINA

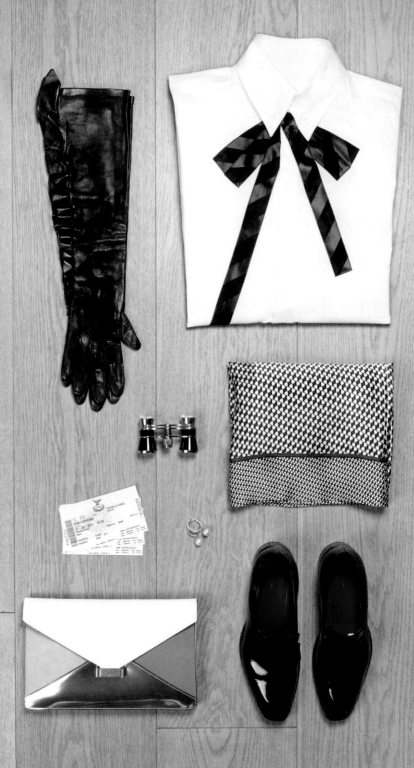

One
of the few sanctuaries for old
aristocratic traditions is
Society.

SNELL ROUNDHAND

Top hats, cummerbunds, patent
leather shoes, and coats with tails are all
remnants of the eighteenth century,
when countries were run by
kings and queens who spoke French to
each other and their entourages.

SNELL ROUNDHAND

NOT

FF SCALA JEWELS

much of that remains, except for maîtres
d'hôtel at posh restaurants who fake French
accents and wear coats with tails.

KÜNSTLER SCRIPT

OF COURSE

MRS. EAVES

French is still the official language
of the diplomatic corps. Typographically speaking,
we have reminders of these somewhat
antiquated traditions in the accepted and expected ways
of designing invitations and programs.

MRS. EAVES ITALIC

CENTERED TYPE AND

A PREFERENCE FOR FONTS THAT COME

FROM A GOOD BACKGROUND IN

COPPER ENGRAVING OR

UPPER CRUST CALLIGRAPHY.

COPPERPLATE

And, of course,

MATRIX SCRIPT INLINE

those very familiar four letters, »rsvp«, which mean
»please let us know whether you're going to be there,«
but actually stand for »Répondez s'il vous plaît.«

SUBURBAN LIGHT

There is no category known as "formal fonts," but a number of typefaces come from that background. The text at the left is set in Snell Roundhand, a formal script from the 1700s, redesigned in 1965 by Matthew Carter.

Apart from formal scripts such as Snell, Künstler Script, and others like it, there are the aptly named copperplates. They look formal and distinguished and are even available in a range of weights and versions, but they all lack one important feature: lowercase characters.

Other typefaces that owe their appearance to the process of engraving into steel as opposed to writing with a quill or cutting into wood are Walbaum, Bauer Bodoni, or ITC Fenice. They can look formal and aristocratic enough to make a favorable impression when printed on fine paper.

While FF Scala Jewels is an extension of the FF Scala family by Martin Majoor from 1993, which is a contemporary interpretation of classic book typefaces, Mrs. Eaves is Zuzana Licko's idiosyncratic take on Baskerville, as seen from Berkeley, California in 1996. It is named after Sarah Eaves, the woman who became John Baskerville's wife. Licko's Matrix Script Inline from 1992 gets closer to American vernacular, and Rudy VanderLans' 1993 Suburban connects classic scripts with, well, suburban neon signs. And, as VanderLans proudly proclaims, Suburban is the only typeface in existence today that uses an upside down *l* as a *y*.

FUTURA

on the town

LYON TEXT

Going out on the town allows us to do the things
we don't get to do in the office,
and to wear all the trendy stuff that we can never
resist buying but don't really need
on a day-to-day basis.

THEINHARDT

typetrends

What makes typefaces trendy is almost unpredictable – much to the chagrin of the people who have to market them. A corporation, a magazine, a TV channel can pick a typeface, expose it to the public, and a new typographic fashion can be born. But, like with fashion and pop music, it usually takes more than one designer in the right place at the right time picking the right font off a web site or out of a catalog.

FF DIN /
FF DIN CONDENSED

There are typefaces that are only suitable for the more <u>occasional occasion.</u> They might be too hip to be used for mainstream communication, or they could simply be too uncomfortable – a bit like wearing very tight jeans rather than admitting that they don't fit us any longer. Very often these offbeat fonts are both – tight in the crotch and extroverted.

Typography is as much a mirror of what goes in society as the styling of cell phones or cars. Cars still take half a dozen years from concept to production, so their designers have to anticipate trends. As cars are the icons of our mobile society, their design, in turn, does create trends. While technology allows us to produce a font in weeks – if not hours – from rough sketches or ideas, it still takes a few years for a typeface to get to market and to the attention of the font-buying public. Right now, early in the 21st century, we are seeing a return to the time-honored classics and their modern interpretations. We have also learned to live with bitmaps, both as a necessity and as a fashion statement. Most industrial type-styles have been exploited, from monospaced typewriter faces through electronic font generators to industrial signage. And some of the most used typefaces were first produced for the signs above or freeways. Interstate is Tobias Frere-Jones' interpretation of the white-on-green letters in the USA, while FF Din expands the model used on Germany's autobahn. Ironically, if a typeface has been designed for one particular purpose, it seems to look really good on anything else.

INTERSTATE BOLD CONDENSED

FUNFONTS

INTERSTATE LIGHT

The entertainment value of this sort of typographical work is often higher than that of the straightforward corporate stuff, so there's a great deal of satisfaction gained not only from the words, but also from the fun of being able to work with really unusual fonts.

GRAPHIK

Fashionable faces

NEUE HELVETICA 75

One thing leather jackets have on trendy typefaces is that the jackets get better as they get older, which is more than can be said about some of the typefaces we loved in the 1980s but would be too embarrassed to ask for now. Like all fashions, however, they keep coming back. Don't throw away your old fonts – keep them for your kids.

BROADWAY LINE AND·STREET

TO 8TH STREET

METROPOLITAN AV

GRAND STREET

23RD · STREET

CLINTON-
WASHINGTON AV

LORIMER·ST

14TH AVE

PENN. STATION

TO CROSSTOWN LINE

As long as you print on paper, the choice of typeface is first and foremost governed by the content of the message, then the intended audience, and only lastly by technical constraints.

Architectural type has to compromise between materials and legibility. A mosaic made up of millions of pieces would allow for smoother letter-shapes, but would neither be as durable nor as affordable as one with coarser bits.

When we move from almost limitless resolution on paper to images generated by cathod rays or liquid crystals, we enter a world of optical illusions. Those have to make up for the lack of high fidelity and trick our eyes into seeing life-like images rather than spots of colored light (see page 132). On the screen, colors are not mixed from CMYK: cyan, yellow, magenta, and black (the k really stands for key), but are broken down into RGB: red, green, and blue; letters are composed of course lines or dots, and black is not an ink, but the absence of light. Typefaces have to work very hard under these conditions. There is no room here for leisure fonts, nor for scripts or some of the trendy faces that hide more than they reveal. The workhorses for "old" media work well in the new. Rugged construction, clear counter spaces, easily discernible figures and well defined weights have all been mentioned before as being prerequisites for anything which has to be read under less than ideal circumstances. And whatever progress technology brings in the future – staring into light coming from a screen is not what human eyes were made for.

All those minute details that make a good typeface pleasant to behold and easy to read, actually add noise. The absence of these details would make the type look cold and technical, as if generated by machines and legible only for machines.

The designer of typefaces suitable for on-screen reading has to balance the requirements of the precise but cold medium (light emitted by all sorts of tubes, crystals, diodes, and plasms) against our need for subtle contrast and soft shapes. And as most of what we read on screen eventually gets printed as well, these alphabets have to offer enough traditional beauty for us to accept them against the competition we've grown used to over 500 years.

Slightly extended lettershapes have more open counters and are thus more legible, but need more space. Subtle contrast between thin horizontals and thicker verticals doesn't translate well into single pixels and tiny serifs may look delicate in display sizes, but on a screen will only add noise at 10pt or less.

The screen fonts offered by Microsoft and Apple work well under all circumstances, but have become too ubiquitous to lend an individual note.

Matthew Carter's Verdana has become a very successful face on paper as well, while Bigelow & Holmes' Lucida, initially designed for laser-printers in 1983, looks also great in high-resolution and is one of the best screen fonts around. FF Typestar by Steffen Sauerteig has those rugged shapes reminiscent of typewriter faces and suited for rough conditions on screen or paper.

Handgloves
Look at these faces at very small sizes and you get an idea of how they will perform on screen.

Handgloves
Look at these faces at very small sizes and you get an idea of how they will perform on screen.

Handglove
Look at these faces at very small sizes and you get an idea of how they will perform on screen.

And if a text is mainly meant for the screen and for very small sizes, pure bitmap fonts work well. If you print them, the pixels are small enough to all but disappear. This is 7pt Tenacity Condensed, a bitmap font from Joe Gillespie.

Brands have to speak their own authentic language. Type is visible language. Using a bland or overused typeface will make the brand and its products or media equally bland and even invisible. Having an exclusive typeface designed or adapted used to be expensive, technically challenging, and difficult to implement. Not anymore. Whether it's just one weight for a packaged product or a large system for everything, corporate fonts have become a major source of work for type designers.

Some companies take an existing face and simply change the name to make it more identifiable – license models exist for that purpose. While they're at it, they often add their logo or other glyphs that can then be accessed via the keyboard. And if the chairman (or his wife) doesn't like the shape of a certain character, that can also be adapted. All with the blessing and preferably the involvement of the original type designer. As a lot of these people are no longer available (think Bodoni, Caslon, or Garamond), the foundry that has the license for the particular typeface will be happy to help.

In 1990, Kurt Weidemann designed a trilogy of faces for Mercedes-Benz that was, in fact, a comprehensive system for all their brands and subbrands. Corporate A stands for Antiqua, the serif version for the car brand; S is Sans, intended for the trucks division; and E is Egyptienne, the slab typeface for the engineering group. This was the first typographic tribe, a family of families. It is no longer exclusive to Mercedes-Benz, so every backstreet garage can now have at least a premium name over the door.

Handgloves
CORPORATE A

Handgloves
CORPORATE S

Handgloves
CORPORATE E

Silicon Valley Bank took the easier route: they chose FF Unit and FF Unit Slab, changed the name for easier recognition, and got a license to distribute it to their suppliers and branches.

Handgloves
SVB SANS

Handgloves
SVB SLAB

When General Electrics started work on its new brand position in 2004, it commissioned an exclusive typeface to express the new direction, perhaps too transparently named GE Inspira. It works well for a large company that makes everything from jet engines to lightbulbs.

Handgloves
GE INSPIRA REGULAR

Handgloves
GE INSPIRA BOLD

svb >
Silicon Valley Bank
Brand Guidelines
Basic Elements

No, Watson, this was not done by accident, but by design.

Monotype Baskerville

Sherlock Holmes is a fictional detective created by Sir Arthur Conan Doyle (1859–1930). Holmes' extraordinary powers of deductive reasoning carry him, along with his somewhat befuddled partner Dr. Watson, through some of the most complex mysteries in detective fiction.

CHAPTER 5

TYPE BUILDS CHARACTER.

FF Unit Regular Small Caps

The Way to Wealth

BENJAMIN FRANKLIN

IF TIME IS OF ALL THINGS the most precious, wasting time must be the greatest prodigality; since lost time is never found again, and what we call time enough always proves too little. Let us then be up and doing, and doing to a purpose, so by diligence we should do more with less perplexity. Sloth makes all things difficult, but industry all things easy. He that riseth late must trot all day and shall scarce overtake the business at night; while laziness travels so slowly that poverty soon overtakes him. Sloth, like rust, consumes faster than labor wears, while the used key is always bright. Do not squander time, for that's the stuff life is made of; how much more than is necessary do we spend in sleep, forgetting that the sleeping fox catches no poultry, and that there will be sleeping enough in the grave.

So what signifies wishing and hoping for better times? We may make these times better if we bestir ourselves. Industry need not wish, and he that lives upon hope will die fasting. There are no gains without pains and he that has a trade has an estate, and he that has a calling has an office of profit and honor. But then the trade must be worked at and the calling well followed. Though you have found no treasure, nor has any rich relation left you a legacy, diligence is the mother of good luck, and all things are given to industry. Plow deep while sluggards sleep, and you will have corn to sell and keep; work while it is called today or you know not how much you may be hindered tomorrow: one today is worth two tomorrows, and farther: have you something to do tomorrow, do it today.

Be ashamed to catch yourself idle. When you have so much to do, be up by the peep of day. Let not the sun look down and say: "Inglorious here he lays." Handle your tools without mittens; remember, that the cat in gloves catches no mice. It is true there is much to be done, and perhaps you are weak-handed, but stick to it steadily, and you will see great effects, for constant dropping wears away stones; and by diligence and patience, the mouse ate in two the cable. If you want a faithful servant, and one

THE WAY BOOKS ARE read hasn't changed very much over the last 500 years, so the way books look hasn't had to change either. Only the economics have changed, which means that publishers today insist on fitting more type onto a page, and they aren't always prepared to pay for good typesetting, let alone for someone to actually design the inside of a book, and not just its cover. Every additional dollar spent on the manufacture of a book adds seven or more dollars to its retail price.

The left hand pages in this chapter have been reduced to fit into this book; most are about two-thirds their optimum size.

Cheap paperbacks, therefore, do not usually represent the state of the typographic art. In general, they could be nicer than they are because it costs no more to observe the basic rules of book layout using a good, legible typeface than to ignore these rules and set the text in whatever the printer happens to have around.

With the arrival of electronic books, cheap paperbacks are on their way out. Unfortunately, type in e-books follows that bad tradition, although good typography wouldn't cost a penny extra.

To show just how much type can accomplish and how versatile it is, we have used the same text, written by Benjamin Franklin in 1733, to set all the samples in this chapter; some liberties have been taken with Mr. Franklin's words to make typographic points.

Our example is set in Adobe Caslon, Carol Twombly's 1990 version of one of the most popular of all the book faces (originally designed by William Caslon in 1725); we also use the Adobe Caslon Expert set (see page 113). The Irish playwright George Bernard Shaw insisted that all his books be set in Caslon, earning him the title "Caslon man at any rate." For decades, the motto of British printers was, "When in doubt, set it in Caslon."

The layout follows the classic model with wide margins, generous space between lines, and a centered title. To achieve a nice, smooth edge on both sides of the column, the punctuation is hung in the right hand margin.

Handgloves

ADOBE CASLON PRO REGULAR

Handgloves

ADOBE CASLON PRO SEMIBOLD

HANDGLOVES

ADOBE CASLON PRO CAPS

ADOBE CASLON ORNAMENTS

Handgloves

ADOBE CASLON PRO ITALIC

Frugality will never go out of style.

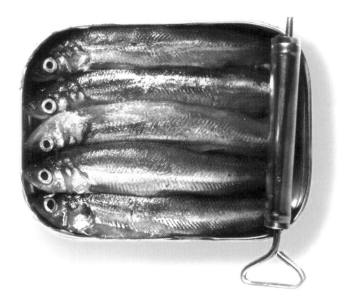

To be secure, certainty and success rely on a dependable financial institution.

It's easy to think that a little tea or a little punch now and then, a diet a little more costly, clothes a little finer, and a little entertainment is no great matter. But at the Bank of Benjamin we think that being aware of small expenses is just as important as the consideration it takes, say, to purchase a home: small leaks will surely sink a great ship. Our financial advisors will always be available to advise the best ways to put your savings to work. We know that what often appears to be a terrific investment quite frequently turns out otherwise. So when confronted by a great pennysworth, our advisors will pause a while: Cheapness is apparent only, and not real. We want our customers to enjoy their hard-earned leisure without having to think about their hard-earned dollars. So be sure to keep this in mind: if you won't listen to reason, it will rap your knuckles.

The Bank of Benjamin

Our advisors are at your service 24 hours a day. Please call us:

1-800-SAVINGS

There also seems to be a generic style for advertisements. Although display advertising does not have a lengthy tradition (it has only been around about 150 years), its style is as established as that of the traditional book. Headline on top, attention-grabbing picture underneath, subhead, main copy, logo, pay-off line, address, URL, or telephone number.

Never more than eight elements! People are able to comprehend at most about that many different components in one message; as soon as there are more, comprehension requires too much effort, and attention goes elsewhere. You can also recognize a serious, idea-based advertisement by the serious typography. No experiments here – take a classic, well-tried typeface, arrange it in a predictable layout, and people may actually read your message.

What is more no-nonsense than Futura, the typeface made respectable in those first VW ads from the 1950s and 1960s? They were truly revolutionary, using this cool, restrained German typeface to promote that strange little car.

Futura is still one of the most popular typeface families, providing art directors all over the world with some of the best bold, extra bold, and condensed fonts available. Advertising certainly wouldn't be the same without Futura.

When Paul Renner started work on Futura in 1924, it was proclaimed as the "typeface for our time," alluding to the social democratic reform of German society in the 1920s. The first weight was released in 1927.

Handgloves — FUTURA LIGHT
Handgloves — FUTURA LIGHT OBLIQUE
Handgloves — FUTURA CONDENSED LIGHT
Handgloves — FUTURA CONDENSED LIGHT OBLIQUE
Handgloves — FUTURA
Handgloves — FUTURA OBLIQUE
Handgloves — FUTURA CONDENSED
Handgloves — FUTURA CONDENSED OBLIQUE

Handgloves — FUTURA BOOK
Handgloves — FUTURA BOOK OBLIQUE
Handgloves — FUTURA HEAVY
Handgloves — FUTURA HEAVY OBLIQUE
Handgloves — FUTURA BOLD
Handgloves — FUTURA BOLD OBLIQUE
Handgloves — FUTURA CONDENSED BOLD
Handgloves — FUTURA CONDENSED BOLD OBLIQUE
Handgloves — FUTURA EXTRA BOLD
Handgloves — FUTURA EXTRA BOLD OBLIQUE
Handgloves — FUTURA CONDENSED EXTRA BOLD
Handgloves — FUTURA COND. EXTRA BOLD OBLIQUE

TIME LINE

a lecture by Frank Franklin

If time is the most precious of all things, wasting time must be the greatest sin. Lost time is never found again, and what we call enough time is never enough. Let us then be up and doing, and doing with a purpose, so by diligence we should do more with less perplexity. Sloth makes all things difficult, but industry all things easy. He that riseth late must trot all day and shall scarce overtake the business at night; while laziness travels so slowly that poverty soon overtakes him. Do not squander time, for that's the stuff life is made of; how much more than is necessary do we spend in sleep, forgetting that the sleeping fox catches no poultry, and that there will be sleeping enough in the grave.

7:00 p.m.

Saturday, December 12

PacBell Park

Remember this, however, if you won't be counseled, you can't be helped, and further: If you will not listen to reason, it will surely rap your knuckles.

He that riseth late must trot all day and shall scarce overtake the business at night.

You may think, perhaps, that a little tea, or a little punch now and then, diet a little more costly, clothes a little finer, and a little entertainment now and then, can be no great matter. Watch those little expenses, a small leak will sink a great ship, and moreover, fools make feasts, and wise men eat them. Buy what you have no need for and before long you shall sell your necessities. Many a one, for the sake of finery on the back have gone with a hungry belly. Silks and satins, scarlet and velvets, put out the kitchen fire. By these and other extravagances the genteel are reduced to poverty.

If you won't be counseled you can't be helped.

The computer has given us access to a design language that would have been far too complicated without the aid of sophisticated programs and a page description language such as PostScript. Gradations of color, overlaid images, frames, lines, boxes, background, foreground – all add up to the appearance of the page as one image, rather than a linear sequence of elements. This particular layout at the left can be classified as "New Wave, ca 1987." The availability of millions of images and thousands of fonts (not to mention 16.7 millions of colors) at the click of a mouse seem to make every perceivable style and fashion – past and future – easy to emulate, if not invent.

Luckily for professional designers, this sounds easier than it is. If everybody could be a successful designer by following simple recipes, we'd be out of work tomorrow. But that extra ingredient, a concept, an idea, cannot be formulated as readily as this. The waves may come and go, but graphic design will always be about problem solving first, and style-making afterward.

For this exercise, I have not shown everything I could on a page. I haven't gone crazy with sampling images, overlaying them as if there were no tomorrow, or using the weirdest fonts available.

Instead, I've picked the typeface that has pretty much replaced Helvetica as Corporate World Font Number One. Frutiger (see page 67) is now available in a good range of weights and widths, making it suitable for almost every typographic task. It avoids Helvetica's blandness, adding instead a humanist touch. This improves legibility by keeping letter shapes open and more distinct from one another.

The condensed weights are particularly suitable for projects that need a clean-looking, highly legible, relatively neutral, and space-saving typeface.

Comparison of critical letter shapes in Akzidenz Grotesk, the mother of most modern sans serifs; Helvetica, the face without features; Univers, the cool alternative; Frutiger, the friendly sans; and Thesis, the typeface with 144 cousins in one family.

aces   BERTHOLD AKZIDENZ GROTESK

aces   HELVETICA

aces   LINOTYPE UNIVERS

aces   FRUTIGER

aces   THESIS

Handgloves
FRUTIGER 45 LIGHT

Handgloves
FRUTIGER 55 ROMAN

Handgloves
FRUTIGER 65 BOLD

Handgloves
FRUTIGER 75 BLACK

Handgloves
FRUTIGER 95 ULTRABLACK

Handgloves
FRUTIGER 57 ROMAN CONDENSED

Handgloves
FRUTIGER 67 BOLD CONDENSED

Handgloves
FRUTIGER 77 BLACK CONDENSED

Handgloves
FRUTIGER 87 EXTRABLACK COND.

Industry need not wish; if you live on hope you will die fasting.
If you have a trade, you have an estate, and if you have a calling you have an office of profit and honor.

*I*f time is the most precious of all things, wasting time must be the greatest sin; since lost time is never found again, and what wecall enough time always proves to be too little. Let's be up and doing, and with a purpose, so by diligence we can do more with less perplexity.

Sloth makes all things difficult, but industry all things easy. If you get up late you must trot all day and barely may overtake the business at night; while laziness travels so slowly that poverty will soon overtake you. Sloth, like rust, consumes faster than labor wears, while the used key is always bright. Time is the stuff life is made of; how much more than is necessary do we spend in sleep, forgetting that the sleeping fox catches no poultry, and that there will be sleeping enough in the grave.

Industry need not wish, if you live on hope you will die fasting. If you have a trade, you have an estate, and if you have a calling you have an office of profit and honor. But then the trade must be worked at and the calling well followed.

Susanna M. Franklin
Chief Executive Officer

Though you have found no treasure, nor has any rich relation left you a legacy, diligence is the mother of good luck, and all things are given to industry. Plow deep while sluggards sleep, and you will have corn to sell and keep; work while it is called today or you know not how much you may be hindered tomorrow: one today is worth two tomorrows, and furthermore: if you have something to do tomorrow, do it today. If you want a faithful servant, and one that you like, serve yourself. Be circumspect and caring, even in the smallest matters, because sometimes a little neglect breeds great mischief: for want of a nail the shoe was lost, for want of a shoe the horse was lost, being soon overtaken and stolen by the enemy.

Pension Assets Exceed $12 Billion

So much for industry, and attention to one's own business, but to these we must add frugality, if we would make our industry more successful. We think of saving as well as of getting. You may think, perhaps, that a little tea, or a little punch now and then, a diet that's a little more costly, clothes

Corporations spend a good deal of money to show their shareholders, their customers, and their banks how good they are (the corporations, not the others). So they hire designers or advertising agencies (there is a difference) to design brochures, booklets, and annual reports to make them look as excellent as they wish they were.

Strangely enough, as anyone who's ever been on a design jury judging annual reports or other corporate messages can attest, many of these printed pieces come out looking very similar. Although some designers set trends and others follow them, they all get paid to make their clients look different from the competition.

It is, therefore, easy enough to design a typically corporate page, at least for the USA. In Europe, this page would look quite different, but with definite similarities within certain countries. You can always tell a German report from a Dutch, British, or Italian one, but they all have one thing in common: the picture of the chairman (or chairwoman).

Judging from the typeface used, the page on the left must be for a financial or similar institution. It is set in Bodoni, and the layout combines classic elements, such as the centered sidebar, with traditional advertising conventions and justified text across a column that is far too narrow to achieve reasonable word breaks and word spaces (more about that in chapter 7).

While you can't go wrong with Bodoni, you could, however, try a different version now and again. Berthold, Linotype, and Monotype Bodonis are very much alike, whereas Bauer Bodoni has so much contrast between thick and thin lines that it isn't really suitable for small sizes. ITC Bodoni is much better at small sizes than all the others. Its little quirks become visible only at large sizes, which might be desirable, as they will add a little life to your pages.

The Bodonis have grown into a large family – everybody who is anybody in the type world offers a different version. Here are a few of the styles and weights available.

Handgloves
BERTHOLD BODONI LIGHT

Handgloves
BERTHOLD BODONI REGULAR

Handgloves
ITC BODONI SEVENTY TWO

Handgloves
ADOBE BODONI BOOK

Handgloves
BAUER BODONI BOLD

Handgloves
ADOBE BODONI ROMAN

Handgloves
BERTHOLD BODONI MEDIUM

Handgloves
ITC BODONI BOLD SIX

Handgloves
BAUER BODONI BOLD

Handgloves
ADOBE BODONI BOLD

Handgloves
ITC BODONI BOLD TWELVE

Handgloves
BAUER BODONI BLACK

Handgloves
BAUER BODONI BLACK CONDENSED

Handgloves
BODONI POSTER COMPRESSED

Alabama
Alaska
Arizona
Arkansas
California
Colorado
Conneticut
Delaware
Florida
Georgia
Hawaii
Idaho
Illinois
Indiana
Iowa
Kansas
Kentucky
Louisiana
Maine
Maryland
Massachusetts
Michigan
Minnesota
Mississippi
Missouri
Montana
Nebraska
Nevada
New Hampshire
New Jersey
New Mexico
New York
North Carolina
North Dakota
Ohio
Oklahoma
Oregon
Pennsylvania
Rhode Island
South Carolina
South Dakota
Tennessee
Texas
Utah
Vermont
Virginia
Washington
West Virginia
Wisconsin
Wyoming

Sales Tax

We are required to collect sales tax on shipments to the states listed at left. Please add the correct percentage amount. If you pay by credit card and don't know your sales tax, leave the line blank and we will fill in the correct amount.

▶ *Time as a Tool*. Benny Frank. Philadelphia: Caslon Publishing, 2002. **790pp. Hardcover. $29.95.**
From Time as a Tool: "If time is the most precious of all things, wasting time must be the greatest sin; since lost time is never found again, and what we call time enough always proves too little. Do not squander time, for that's the stuff life is made of; how much more than is necessary do we spend in sleep, forgetting that the sleeping fox catches no poultry, and that there will be sleeping enough in the grave."

▶ *Circumspection at Work*. Fran Benjamin. Philadelphia: Caslon Publishing, 2002. **145pp. Softcover. $12.95.**
From Circumspection at Work: "So what signifies wishing and hoping for better times? We could make these times better if we bestir ourselves. Industry need not wish, and he that lives upon hope will die fasting. There are no gains without pains. If you have a trade you have an estate, and if you have a calling you have an office of profit and honor. But then the trade must be worked at and the calling well followed. Though you have found no treasure, nor has any rich relation left you no legacy, diligence is the mother of good luck, and all things are given to industry. Plow deep while sluggards sleep, and you will have corn to sell and keep; work while it is called today or you know not how much you may hindered tomorrow: one today is worth two tomorrows, and farther: have you something to do tomorrow, do it today."

▶ *Time & Saving*. Jamie Franklin. Philadelphia: Caslon Publishing, 2003. **220 pp. Softcover. $12.95.**
From Time & Saving: "We must consider frugality, if we want to make our work more certainly successful. A person may, if she doesn't know how to save as she gets, keep her nose all her life to the grindstone, and die not worth a penny at the last. A fat kitchen does make a lean will. Think of saving as well as of getting. A small leak will sink a great ship. Cheapness is apparent only, and not real; the bargain, by straitening you in business, might do you more harm than good. 'At a great pennyworth, pause awhile.'"

Ordering Information

Name

Address

City	**State**	**Zip**	**Country**

Telephone	**E-Mail**

Book Title	**Quantity**
Book Title	**Quantity**
Book Title	**Quantity**

Subtotal

Sales Tax

Shipping (please add $2 per book)

Total Order

Method of Payment

Check or money order enclosed, payable to TimeSaving Books Ltd.

Please charge my credit card

Credit Card Number	**Expiration Date**
Visa/MasterCard	American Express

Signature (required for credit card purchases)

One of the areas typographers usually stay well clear of is the design of forms. They are not the easiest things to design, and in that respect should be considered a challenge. They offer enormous rewards – not winning awards or being included in the design annuals, but in terms of achievement.

Forms always have too much copy, so first choose a font that is narrower than your run-of-the-mill ones. Make sure it is clearly legible, has a good bold weight for emphasis, and has readable numerals.

Keep the preprinted information clearly separated from the areas you want people to fill in. These lines should be inviting guides for people's handwriting, and not look like bars on a prison cell window. The same can be said of boxes around text. Who needs them? Some designers seem to be afraid that the type might fall off the page if there isn't a box around it: it won't happen! Without restricting boxes, forms don't look half as forbidding and official. Different areas on the page can be separated by white space, as shown in our example.

If any typeface was designed to be neutral, clean, and practical, it is Univers, designed by Adrian Frutiger, 1957. The condensed versions of this typeface are actually quite legible, considering how much copy can fit into a confined space.

Forty years later, Linotype started work on a new version of Frutiger's original design. The family now includes 59 weights plus four monospaced typewriter weights. While the old system featured a numerical system to distinguish the weights, with Univers 55 being the normal roman weight, the new Linotype Univers needs three digits. Basic regular is now 430. The first digit stands for weight, i.e., 1 is ultralight, 2 thin, etc., and 9 is extra black. The second digit denotes width, i.e., 1 for compressed, 2 for condensed, 3 for basic, and 5 for extended. The third indicates upright roman (0) or italic (1). Not exactly intuitive, but effective once you get used to it. Frutiger, Neue Helvetica, Centennial, and a few other Linotype faces are still classified according to the old system using two digits to signify weight and width or slant.

140	141	130	131	120	121	110
240	241	230	231	220	221	210
340	341	330	331	320	321	310
440	441	430	431	420	421	410
540	541	530	531	520	521	510
640	641	630	631	620	621	
740	741	730	731	720	721	
840	841	830	831	820	821	
940	941	930	931	920	921	

This table shows how all the weights of Univers relate to each other. The numbering system makes sense – once you've thought about it.

BY FRANK BENJAMIN

THE TIME IS

NOW!

If time be of all things the most precious, wasting time must be the greatest prodigality; since lost time is never found again, and what we call time enough always proves little enough. Let us then be up and doing, and doing to a purpose, so by diligence we should do more with less perplexity. Sloth makes all things difficult, but industry all things easy. He that riseth late must trot all day and shall scarce overtake the business at night, while soon overtakes him. Sloth, like rust, consumes faster than labor wears, while the used key is always bright. Do not squander time, for that's the stuff life is made of; how much more than is necessary do we spend in sleep, forgetting that the sleeping fox catches no poultry, and that there will be sleeping enough in the grave.

So what signifies wishing and hoping for better times? We may make these times better if we stir ourselves. Industry need not wish, and he that lives upon hope will die fasting. There are no gains without pains. If you have a trade you have an estate, and if you have a calling you have an office of profit and honor. But then the trade must be worked at and the calling well followed. Though you have found no treasure, nor has any rich relation left you a legacy, diligence is the mother of good luck, and all things are given to industry.

> "Wise men learn by others' harms, fools scarcely by their own."

Plow deep while sluggards sleep, and you will have corn to sell and keep; work while it is called today or you know not how much you may be hindered tomorrow: one today is worth two tomorrows, and farther: have you something to do tomorrow, do it today. If you want a faithful servant, and one that you like, serve yourself. Be circumspect and caring, even in the smallest matters, because sometimes a little neglect breeds great mischief: for want of a nail the shoe was lost, for want of a shoe the horse was lost, being soon overtaken and stolen by the enemy, all for want of care of a horseshoe nail. You may think, perhaps, that a little tea, or a little punch now and then, diet a little more costly, clothes a little finer, and little entertainment now and then, can be no great matter: Many a little makes a mickle; beware of little expenses, a small leak will sink a great ship, and again, who dainties love shall.

Magazines are perhaps one of the best indicators of a country's current typographical taste; most of them get redesigned often enough to be on top of contemporary cultural inclinations. Magazine publishing is a very competitive business, and design plays a significant role in the way magazines present themselves to the general public.

Depending on the readership, magazines can look old-fashioned, conservative, pseudoclassic, trendy, cool, technical, newsy, and noisy. All of these signals are conveyed by typography, which may or may not be an adequate representation of the editorial contents.

For our example, we have chosen to combine a very traditional layout with a not-so-traditional typeface. The page employs a lot of the paraphernalia of "good"editorial layout: drop capitals, letterspaced headers, scotch rules, large pullquotes, italic lead-ins, and a contrasting bold sans serif to complement the serif text face. The italic lead-in uses a bit of a gimmick with those diminishing sizes to attract attention and is just trendy enough to appeal to people between thirtysomething and the midlife crisis. These people are reportedly willing to read more than a couple of paragraphs in one sitting.

The textface at left is FF Quadraat by Fred Smeijers. Its almost upright italic and overall condensed letterforms give away its Dutch origin. It is unusual enough to convey a difference, but not so silly and overdesigned as to distract from normal reading.

On close inspection at larger sizes, FF Quadraat looks as strange as the double *a* in its name. Since it was intended to be set in between 7 and 12 point for long copy and continuous reading, those seemingly exaggerated traits add up to character. No slick mechanical precision here, which may look cold to our eyes, but little quirks to delight the tired eye. Smeijers made thorough studies of hand punchcutting techniques and cut punches himself before he used the computer to digitize his drawings. In fact, he has written a book on the subject, called *Counterpunch*.

Franklin Gothic was also cut in steel punches back in 1904 when Morris Fuller Benton first designed the face for ATF. It, too, has kept a liveliness that is often missing from digital fonts. The little eccentricities helped to make Franklin Gothic the proverbial Anglo-Saxon sans serif. Even today, there are not many other typefaces that combine impact and friendliness as well.

Handgloves

QUADRAAT REGULAR

Handgloves

QUADRAAT BOLD

Handgloves

QUADRAAT SANS

Handgloves

QUADRAAT SANS CONDENSED

Handgloves

QUADRAAT DISPLAY

Handgloves

FRANKLIN GOTHIC CONDENSED

Handgloves

FRANKLIN GOTHIC EXTRA COND.

Handgloves

ITC FRANKLIN GOTHIC DEMI

Good Times, Better Times

> "Inglorious
> here he lays."
> **Francis Franklin**

Wishing and hoping for better times? We can make these times better if we bestir ourselves.

Industry need not wish, and if you live upon hope you will die fasting.
If you have a trade, you have an estate, and if you are lucky enough to have a calling,
you have an office of profit and honor. But the trade must be
worked at and the calling well followed. Though you have found no treasure,
nor has any rich relation left you a legacy, remember that diligence is the mother
of good luck, and all things are given to industry.
Work while it is called today because you don't know
how much you may hindered tomorrow:

NEW!

Be ashamed to catch yourself idle. When you have so much to do, be up by the peep of day. Handle your tools without mittens; remember, that the cat in gloves catches no mice. There is much to be done, and perhaps you are weak-handed, but stick to it, and you will see great effects, for constant dropping wears away stones; and by diligence and patience, the mouse ate in two the cable and allow me to add, little strokes fell great oaks. If you want a faithful servant, and one that you like, serve yourself.

Be circumspect and caring, even in the smallest matters, because sometimes a little neglect breeds great mischief. For want of a nail the shoe was lost, for want of a shoe the horse was lost, being soon overtaken and stolen by the enemy, all for want of a horseshoe nail. So much for industry, and attention to one's own business, but we must add frugality to these if we want to make our industry more successful.

Today's lifestyle has one thing going for it: it provides tomorrow's nostalgia; as soon as things are far enough down memory lane, we invariably start looking at them with enchanted eyes.

The other good thing about nostalgia is that you can recycle ideas without being accused of petty larceny; people might even admire your interest in things historical. Frederic Goudy once said "The old guys stole all our best ideas"– we could certainly do worse than look to the past for typographic inspiration. After all, most of the typeface styles we now see have been around for a few hundred years, or at least several decades.

Old advertisements are always a source of amusement, and today we have access to digital versions of the typefaces our predecessors used. We can re-create early ads almost faithfully. A note of caution: if you imitate that old look too well, people might not realize that you're actually trying to tell (or sell) them something new.

The fonts used in our nostalgic ad all go back to the days of hot metal typesetting, when one typeface would have to serve the printer not only for setting advertisements, but also for things like invitations and stationery. Type was neither cheap nor as easily available as it is today, so a printer's investment had to go a long way. Letterpress printing meant that letters literally got pressed, and that pressure would leave its mark; the finer the type, the more it would show wear and tear. Jobbing fonts, as they were called, had to be strong enough to withstand the mechanical pressure and loud enough to be noticed. And being somewhat condensed to save precious space was certainly a bonus.

Every foundry had its own version of these hardworking typefaces. Hermes from Schriftguss AG was first produced around 1908, as was its twin, Berthold's Block. In the USA, William Hamilton Page patented his wood type in 1887. They all show a similar approach to the problem: blunt corners, low contrast, and soft outlines. If a letter already looked a little worn, one wouldn't notice the effects of bad treatment as obviously as one would with a sharp Bodoni, for example.

Rhode is David Berlow's successful attempt to combine early English Grotesques, as made by Figgins at the beginning of the nineteenth century, and American advertising type, like the straight-sided Railroad Gothic, into a complete and large family of sans serifs. Quiet it is not, but it has great presence.

Matthew Butterick rendered four weights of his version of Hermes in 1995. It has the smudges of rough presswork built into the design itself. Hamilton was adapted by Tom Rickner in 1993. He followed the original Bold weight and used it as the basis for his medium and light versions. While Hamilton Bold is already quite condensed, the Medium and the Light certainly don't waste any space with open counters or too-tall ascenders.

Handgloves
BERLINER GROTESK LIGHT

Handgloves
BLOCK REGULAR

HANDGLOVES
FF GOLDEN GATE GOTHIC

met and de of for het und
FF CATCH WORDS

HANDGLOVES
FF PULLMAN INLINE

Handgloves
RHODE BLACK CONDENSED

Handgloves
RHODE BOLD CONDENSED

Handgloves **Handgloves** **Handgloves**
HAMILTON LIGHT, MEDIUM, BOLD

Hand Hand **Hand** **Handgloves**
HERMES THIN, REGULAR, BOLD, BLACK

THE

DAILY INTEREST

Largest Circulation Anywhere

NATIONAL

Boy Raised by $ea Otters Declared Financial Wizard

Be ashamed to catch yourself idle. When you have so much to do, be up by the peep of day. Don't let the sun look down and say: «Inglorious here she lays.» Handle those tools without mittens; remember, that the cat in gloves catches no mice. It is so true there is much to be done, and perhaps you are weak-handed, but stick to it steadily, and you will see great effects, for constant dropping wears away stones; and by diligence and patience, the mouse ate in two the cable, and little strokes fell great oaks. If you want a faithful servant, and one that you like, serve yourself. Be cicumspect and caring, even in the smallest matters, because sometimes a little neglect breeds great mischief: for want of a nail the shoe was lost, for want of a shoe the horse was lost, being soon overtaken and stolen by the enemy, all for want of care of a horseshoe nail.   *pg. 12*

Aliens Open $1 Million Account in Tucson

EXCLUSIVE

ELVIS SEEN AT BANK

Woman Faints While Waiting for Travelers Cheques: "I thought it was my new diet."

Think of saving as well as getting. A person may, if she doesn't know how to save it as she gets it, keep her nose to the grindstone, and die not worth a penny. A kitchen does makes a lean will. You may think, perhaps that a little tea, or a little punch now and then, a diet th a little more costly, clothes a little finer, and little enterta ment now and then, can be no great matter: Many a li makes a mickle; beware of those little expenses – a sm leak will sink a great ship, and be reminded again those who love dainties shall beggars prove, and mo over, fools make feasts, and wise men eat them. Buy w you don't need and before long you will sell your nece ties. «At a great pennyworth, pause awhile.» Cheapnes apparent only, and not real; the bargain, by straiten you in business.   *continued on p*

Every society needs a diversion that doesn't do any physical harm, but keeps those people who prefer to live in fantasy worlds occupied. Certain newspapers cater to this segment of the populace, and the typographic styles reflect their journalistic attitude toward the truth. How do you design stories about children born with three heads, or families that glow in the dark, or nine-month-old babies who can bench-press their moms? Easy: take bold, preferably condensed typefaces, randomly distort the shapes electronically, put outlines around them, mix several together, and insert on the same page.

We haven't quite dared to apply the same techniques in this book. Neither have we exposed our readers to the sort of illustrations these sensationalist newspapers use, although image-manipulation has never been so easy with such realistic results: it's almost too simple to depict a UFO hovering over West Virginia.

Once you start looking for really bold condensed fonts, you realize that there can never be enough of these, as every magazine needs headlines that shout and scream. We mentioned the ever-present Futuras, Franklin Gothics, and Antique Olives on page 53, where we also showed Flyer, Block, and Poplar, as well as some newer alternatives. Most of these, however, are far too well behaved and good looking to use in a sensationalist way.

Handgloves
AACHEN BOLD

Handgloves
FF SARI EXTRA BOLD

Handgloves
FORMATA BOLD CONDENSED

Handgloves
INTERSTATE ULTRA BLACK COND.

Handgloves
GRIFFITH ULTRA CONDENSED

Handgloves
FF FAGO CONDENSED

Handgloves
IMPACT

Handgloves
TEMPO HEAVY CONDENSED

Handgloves
FF UNIT ULTRA

Handgloves
AMPLITUDE EXTRA COMP. ULTRA

Map Projections

These pages describe a number of well-known map projections, and how they are drawn and used. I also include a map projection I designed while at University, circa 1978. It is a conventional projection, neither conformal nor equal-area, which depicts the world on an ellipse with a 3:2 aspect ratio.

Other Topics

Telescopes and eyepieces: a short page explaining how a telescope works, and describing various common types of telescopes and eyepieces.

HTML: A brief summary of HTML, to help you to write your own web page, was added, since this site contains lots of examples, and was created with a text editor (and hence its HTML source code is nice and readable).

Colors: This page contains a couple of pretty color charts. May not display perfectly in 256-color mode.

Signal Flag Systems: This page contains a picture showing the flags used for the International Code of Signals, as used by ships, and the flags from some other signalling systems as well.

An example of a computer architecture, which illustrates how computers work at the machine language level.

A brief discussion of my thoughts on a computer language that is mostly an improved FORTRAN.

Illustrations of a few designs for computer keyboards that have been used through the ages.

And some comments on why I favor big-endian architecture, and how I wish text files should be stored.

Chess: here, I suggest a new approach to explaining some of the rules of chess that confuse beginners, and I propose an extremely modest rule change to chess that might help to improve its interest and popularity without changing it so much as to, in essence, replace it by another game.

The Musical Scale: here, I briefly discuss the integer harmonic ratios that have given rise to the scale used in Western music.

A Space Habitat Design: The problem of secondary radiation from cosmic rays has been claimed to make space habitats, such as those envisaged by Gerard K. O'Neill, impractical. Here is illustrated a design, admittedly less exciting in appearance than designs with large expanses of glass open to space, that can work even if one needs six metres of rock for shielding. The shielding doesn't rotate, so large structural loads are avoided, and consumables are not required to re-orient the structure to the sun on a continuing basis.

Travelling to Mars: I briefly discuss some of the things involved in sending people to Mars, describing the Hohmann orbit, and Dr. Zubrin's Mars Direct proposal and NASA's Mars Reference Mission derived from it.

Lining up the Planets: a brief look at how often the planets line up in a row.

A Tall Building Design: a conventional idea for how a tall building might be made, inspired by the recent construction of many tall buildings around the world.

Movie and TV Aspect Ratios: a field guide to the "black bars" you may see on a TV set when watching widescreen movies in their original form.

A Limitation of Color Photography: I note that color photography, as ordinarily carried out with film, has an intrinsic limitation as regards the control of contrast, and illustrate that it can be solved, and the benefit of doing so.

The page on the left is one of my favorite web pages ever: www.quadibloc.com. Its author, John Savard, is incredibly generous with the knowledge he shares. This is what he says:

"There are many pages on this site concerning various topics of an entertaining, yet somewhat technical, nature that many visitors should find fascinating."

He is a nerd in the best possible way – totally committed to his subject matter. He'd rather spend his time gathering facts and making them available than wasting it on what he probably thinks are unnecessary, even frivolous, cosmetics.

But if he did want to reach out to more people and had the resources of a designer and a coder, his message would be served more effectively.

But then again, it is people like John Savard who make the web what it still can be: a place where knowledge is shared, in the open, for everybody. While his site would never win a design award, I am grateful for the fact that he does not even try to dress it up. It is what it is. What you see is what you get. Not a shining example of communication design, but a generous gift to us all.

Unlike books or magazines, web sites are in landscape format, i.e. wider than tall. The length of a line depends on how far you drag the size of the window on the screen. A one-column layout can yield 200 characters per line – almost impossible to read. Ten words per line would be comfortable, but require a layout with narrower columns.

Color is free on the web. While there's nothing wrong with black text on white, using different colors not only adds a bit of drama to the page, but also creates hierarchies for the content.

A serif face for body copy is appropriate, but a little contrast is always helpful: Captions, headlines, and subheads could use a sans for contrast. There are also plenty of new monospaced fonts around to replace Courier, which tends to look too thin on screen.

We've taken the copy from the page below and made some very simple edits. Two columns make the type easier to read and saves a lot of space, FF Meta Serif is not as spindly as Times, and the code looks good in Fira Mono and in color. A sans serif headline adds contrast and doesn't need to be very big to be noticed. Half lines between paragraphs suffice.

The result still isn't very pretty, but the type is much bigger even though the page now fits more text!

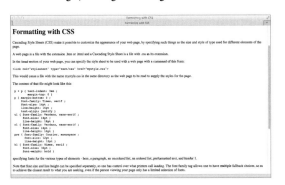

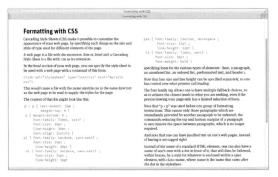

If time be of all things the most precious, wasting time must be the greatest prodigality; |

since lost time is never found again, | and what we call time enough always proves little enough. | Let us then be up and doing, and doing to a purpose,

so by diligence we should do more with less perplexity. | Sloth makes all things difficult, but industry all things easy. |

He that riseth late must trot all day and shall scarce overtake the business at night; while laziness travels so slowly

that poverty soon overtakes him. | Sloth, like rust, consumes faster than labor wears, while the used key is always bright. | Do not squander

time, for that's the stuff life is made of; for how much more than is necessary do we spend in sleep, forgetting that there will be sleeping enough in the grave.

So what signifies wishing and hoping for better times ? | We may make these times better if we bestir ourselves. | Industry need not wish, and

he that lives upon hope will die fasting. | There are no gains without pains. | He that hath a trade

hath an estate. | Though you have found no treasure, nor has any rich relation left you a legacy, diligence is the mother

of good luck, and all things are given to industry. | Plow deep while sluggards sleep and you will have corn.

Although symbol sets are not, strictly speaking, actual typefaces, they are still able to depict Ben Franklin's message accurately. They are widely available and can be used for text, just like letters. In fact, our alphabet started out as pictograms, little drawings symbolizing objects, people, activities, or events.

A drawing of a skull and crossbones is internationally understood as a sign of death or (at least) danger; the arrow indicates direction or movement; a bed is a bed, signifying rest; a clock stands for time, the dollar sign for money.

Generally, symbols, signs, and dingbats are used to express an idea that would take up too much room to say in words, especially if it has to be understood by people from different cultures and therefore be written in more than one language. Airport signage is the obvious example.

It might be appropriate to substitute a symbol for a frequently used word or phrase, or just to add sparkle to the text. There are many symbol fonts available. Often a symbol can be used to good effect quite differently from the way it was intended. And if the symbol you want doesn't exist, just draw it for yourself in an illustration program.

CARTA

POPPI

GLYPHISH

FF BOKKA ONE

FF DINGBATS 2.0

Since we started reading messages and even long text on small screens, designers of these devices had to cram more and more information into very little space. Words are often too long and also need to be translated into many languages which may use from three to 20 or more characters for the same expression. So they went back to those icons that we used before the alphabet was developed into the incredibly concise system that it is today.

Type designers have turned their attention to these icons and made them either to extend a companion typeface or to exist on their own just for UI (User Interface) applications.

An arrow can mean anything. It can pierce a heart to represent love, it can be bent in the middle to represent lightning or to warn of high voltage, it can announce a change of direction or confirm the chosen direction, it can denote a relation between sender and receiver.

This usage ignores the accepted logic of signage systems. There, an arrow points in the direction in which we're supposed to move. The arrow serves as a topological symbol, it indicates our relation to a given area. And because it's so simple, we can also understand when it's used in the sense of "from-to." Indicating left in our left-to-right reading direction can only mean that something is going out.

A lof of typefaces come with arrows. They can be had in different weights, styles, and positions.

Without arrows we'd be lost wherever we go. No signage can function without this archaic sign – concrete yet symbolic – which is much older than our alphabet.

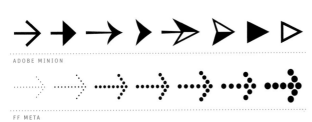

ADOBE MINION

FF META

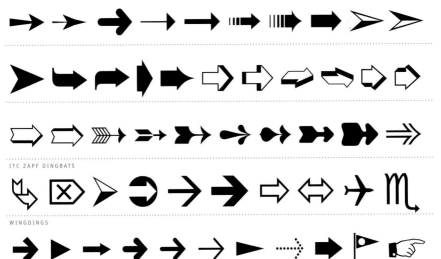

ITC ZAPF DINGBATS

WINGDINGS

FF DINGBATS

Letters are things, not pictures of things.

Eric Gill (1882–1940)
was a sculptor,
carver of inscriptional
lettering, wood
engraver, book illus-
trator, and essayist
on cultural issues.
Gill's eccentric and
controversial per-
sonal style continues
to be a much talked
about and incongruous
element in his list
of considerable
accomplishments. He
designed the type-
faces Gill Sans,
Perpetua, and Joanna.

CHAPTER 6

Types of type.

FF Unit Slab Regular

WHAT DO WE REMEMBER about people? Without the aid of sound and scent, we have to rely on the visual data: the color of their eyes and their hair; are they tall or small, slight or heavy; do they wear glasses, have a beard or crooked teeth?

Many of these features are obscured and thus unavailable for use in identification when somebody steps into your path from the direction of the sun. All you see is a featureless outline. The more clothes this somebody wears, the more the shape is obscured. The worst case is the one illustrated here: we asked John, Paul, George, and Rita to wear hats and jackets for these photographs, and consequently had difficulty telling who was who when we looked at the prints.

But then that was the point. Typographically speaking, this would be like spelling words in capitals only and then putting a box around each letter. You would have to look at each letter individually to be able to spell the word, and there would be no help from the overall word shapes. Unfortunately, many signs that we are supposed to be able to read in passing are designed this way. But words are like faces: the more features we can see, the easier it is to tell who is who.

While we have made things difficult by only using capitals and putting those into a box, we at least used a typeface that is easy to read; the letterforms are distinct enough to be told apart, while not so individual that one has trouble reading complete words.

When we read longer text, we don't look at individual characters; we recognize whole word shapes and see what we expect to see. That's why we don't often spot typing errors. But when we are looking for something new or unknown, like the name of a place or a person, we need to look at each letter carefully. This is particularly true for checking names or numbers in telephone books or other directories. The typefaces designed for these purposes (shown on page 41) give prominence to individual characters. For text fonts, the art is creating clear, distinguishable letterforms that harmonize well in words and sentences.

The big test words in boxes are set in Myriad; below are alternative sans serif capitals.

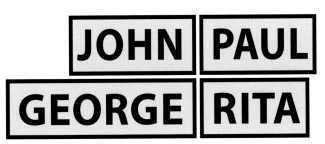

GEORGE
ITC AVANT GARDE GOTHIC DEMI

GEORGE
GILL SANS BOLD

GEORGE
FF DIN BOLD

GEORGE
FUTURA HEAVY

GEORGE
THESIS SANS BOLD

GEORGE
HELVETICA MEDIUM

GEORGE
FF META NORMAL

GEORGE
FF KIEVIT MEDIUM

Since it's polite to take off one's hat when meeting someone, we now have a chance to get a better look at our four well-mannered friends: still no faces, but different hairstyles give us better clues to their identities. Setting the names in capitals and lower case gives each of the words a definite outline.

If you look at them again, you could probably tell them apart just by the shape of the box, at least that is what your unconscious mind will do: if it sees a familiar shape, it will automatically give you the name associated with it.

The outline of a word is determined by which letters jut up from the main body and which hang down. They are called ascenders and descenders, respectively.

Research has shown that our eyes scan the top of the letters' x-heights during the normal reading process, so that is where the primary identification of each letter takes place. The brain assembles the information and compares it with the shape of the word's outline. If we had to consciously look at individual letters all the time, we would read as slowly as children who have not learned to assume a word's meaning from such minimal information.

While ascenders and descenders are vital for easy reading, they have to blend in so they don't attract attention to themselves. Typefaces with exaggerated details may look very attractive word by word, but are their own worst enemies when it comes to unimpeded reading. In typography, everything is connected to everything else; individual elements are noticeable only at the expense of the whole.

The test words on the left are set in capital and lowercase Myriad. Below are ascenders and descenders, as performed by four other typefaces.

George & Paul

Antique Olive (hardly any ascenders or descenders)

George & Paul

ITC Garamond Book (not very explicit)

George & Paul

Stempel Garamond (average)

George & Paul

Weiss Italic (pretty obvious ascenders)

The moment of truth, in life as in typography: no more hiding behind hats or coming in from the light. Now we can look at features – eyes, lips, hair – as well as stylistic additions like glasses and haircuts. And our friends have expressions on their faces, although they were all told to look "normal."

Obviously that meant something different to each of them, as it does when typefaces are described as normal, useful, or sturdy, let alone beautiful, delicate, or handsome.

Most graphic designers and typographers agree that only a handful of typefaces is needed for their daily work; fortunately (at least for the manufacturers and type designers), they could never agree on the same dozen or so typefaces. We need thousands. Then each of us can pick our favorites. Just like shoes: one doesn't need more than half a dozen pairs, but another person will make a different selection, and so on. For individual expression, as well as maximum legibility, we need to pull out all the stops.

Picking the right font for a particular message can be fun, but also extremely difficult. What do you want to express besides the bare facts? How much do you want to interpret, add your own comment, decorate, illustrate? Even if you choose what might be called a "neutral" typeface, you've made a choice that tells people the message is neutral.

When you design the visual appearance of a message, you are adding some interpretation to it. John, Paul, George, and Rita would doubtless have a lively discussion about the typefaces chosen to represent their names and thus, them.

The choices were governed not so much by trying to get across their personalities, as by the actual letters appearing in their names. The choice of a typeface can manipulate the meaning of that word.

John

GILL SANS BOLD

Paul

TEKTON BOLD

George

FF SCALA CONDENSED BOLD

Rita

ITC BENGUIAT GOTHIC BOLD

It is one thing to pick typefaces to represent individual people, and quite another to express similarities as well as differences within the same family. We know that sisters and brothers don't always get along with each other. However, it is easy to tell when people belong to the same family; some take after the father, some after the mother, and some have a combination of both parents' features.

The Von Trapp family demonstrated old-fashioned family values: live together, sing together.

Type also comes in families. While some weights might be used more extensively than others (you wouldn't set a whole book in semibold type), there is no paternal or maternal dominance within typographic families. Each member does its work regardless of age or status. In some respects, the world of type is an ideal one.

Traditionally, typefaces used for setting books had no bold weights, let alone extrabold or condensed versions, or even real display weights. Those more eye-catching additions came about at the beginning of the nineteenth century, when the Industrial Revolution created the need to advertise goods.

Properly applied, however, a complete family gives you enough scope to solve all typographic problems in the setting of text. Nowadays, semibold or bold weights are part of even the most traditional families.

If you find that incestuous typography won't solve your communication problem, you can go outside and bring in some fresh blood from other families. These days, this is quite permissible – more about that on page 121.

The Adobe Garamond family was designed in 1989 by Robert Slimbach. Without its small capitals, and bold and italic children, and its titling cousin, this typographic family wouldn't be large enough to form a choir.

Handgloves
ADOBE GARAMOND REGULAR

Handgloves
ADOBE GARAMOND ITALIC

Handgloves
ADOBE GARAMOND SEMIBOLD

Handgloves
ADOBE GARAMOND SEMIBOLD ITALIC

Handgloves
ADOBE GARAMOND BOLD

Handgloves
ADOBE GARAMOND BOLD ITALIC

HANDGLOVE
ADOBE GARAMOND TITLING

HANDGLOVES
ADOBE GARAMOND SMALL CAPS

Can you tell the difference between a National steel guitar, a square-neck Hawaiian, a Fender Telecaster, a Dreadnought, or an acoustic twelve-string? Look to your left. All of those guitars are there, displayed in the living room of the musician who let us take this photograph. To play a wide variety of music, all of these guitars are used.

Even though only serious musicians could detect the difference between instruments on a recording, the guitarist still has to decide which one will make the particular piece sound perfect, just as a chef will use spices you've never heard of to make your supper taste wonderful. It's the adaptation of one basic, popular tool to serve many different purposes, and the professional needs all the choices available.

When it comes to refinement, type is no exception. Not surprisingly, the fonts providing that extra something are called "expert sets." Some of them do indeed require an expert to find all the right characters and put them in the proper place, but when you have a complex problem to solve, you cannot expect a simple solution.

Today, most OpenType fonts have some of these features integrated, and those with a "Pro" in their name have enough to make even the most demanding type nerd happy.

Remember the typewriter? It has fewer keys than a computer keyboard, and the most you could get on your golfball or daisywheel were 96 characters. Considering that the English alphabet only has 26 letters, that isn't bad, but compare it with the full character set of at least 220 characters in a typical digital font.

There are languages other than English, measurements other than inches, feet, and yards. Specialized professions and sciences require their own ways of encoding and decoding messages, and expert sets make this a little easier. Two types of characters that used to be part of standard typeface families are now found in expert sets: old style figures and ligatures.

Numerals can be an eyesore when they are set in the middle of regular text. Old style figures, sometimes called lowercase figures, are endowed with features like ascenders and descenders, which allow them to blend right in with the other words on a page. Sometimes, a letter collides with a part of a neighboring one. The most obvious example is the overhang on the *f* and the dot on the *i*. Combination characters, called ligatures, prevent that unhappy collision.

ct fb ff fh ffi fi fj fk fl ft sp st Th

ct fb ff fh ffi fi fj fk fl ft sp st Th

Before and after ligatures.

Many special characters deserve a mention in a book about type and typography: the pilcrow, the octothorpe, the ampersand, the @ symbol, asterisk and dagger, hyphen, the en dash, the em dash, &cetera. As it happens, Keith Houston has already written a book about all of them: *Shady Characters*. There is nothing anyone could possibly add to that, so we'll just have to stick with bare essentials here.

When you want to put something into quotes, you usually just press the key with those two short lines on it. On most operating systems, that represents a plain double stroke. Using that instead of proper typographic quotes gives you away as a beginner, a lawyer, a bookkeeper – anything but a professional designer. Proper quotes look like two commas. Depending on the language being set, these can be at the bottom, looking like 99; at the top like 99; at the top reversed, like 66; or at the bottom reversed, like 66. The same goes for single quotes.

Mechanical typewriter keyboards used only very few keystrokes: no option/command/alt-shifts there. There were around 96 keys available, so no room for fancy stuff, just the bare essentials. The inch mark had to act as double quotes and the single foot mark as apostrophe. Some keyboards didn't even have a figure *1*, so you would have to use the lowercase *l* instead. Likewise there were zero zeros – the plain old *O* would have to do.

Sticking with those conventions would be like listening to an old-fashioned transistor radio from the 50s instead of a proper stereo. Same music but increased listening pleasure.

The "dumb" quote was one of the glyphs used to keep down the number of keys on a typewriter. It had to do multiple duties and was used for an apostrophe and closing single quotation mark ('), for an opening quotation mark ('), and for a prime mark ('). Real prime and double prime marks are used to represent feet, hours, inches and minutes. They are almost impossible to find on a computer keyboard. On a US Apple keyboard, type alt+E for a single prime and alt+G for a double.

DIDOT

ADOBE GARAMOND

EQUITY

FF UNIT

LO-TYPE

BLOCK

NEUE HELVETICA

FF DIN

UNIVERS

FUTURA

OPTIMA

PALATINO

FANFARE

REPORTER

MARKER FELT

Applications age very quickly and need to be updated or even replaced almost every season. Fonts, however, which were released decades ago, can still be installed and used. Therefore many users still consider OpenType a disruptive new format, although it's been around since 1996.

OpenType is named appropriately. It works across platforms and operating systems, with its technical specs well hidden under the hood. Programs like the Adobe Creative Suite fully exploit whatever the type designer has included, but you need to look a little deeper.

Expanded character sets and layout features can be fun to use, and linguistic support extends to Greek or Cyrillic characters and even beyond. Stylistic sets offer advanced typographic control but are not always easy to get to. Reading the spec sheets provided by most foundries can reveal a treasure of typographic features that will make layouts look amazingly professional at no extra cost except some investment of time. But who wouldn't enjoy pulling all the stops on stuff like Contextual Alternates or Discretionary Ligatures?

HandHandHandHandHandHandglovesglovesglovesglovesgloves

FF MARK HAIRLINE, THIN, EXTRA LIGHT, LIGHT, REGULAR, BOOK, MEDIUM, BOLD, HEAVY, BLACK

DISCRETIONARY LIGATURES: This feature replaces a sequence of glyphs with a single glyph which, in contrast to the Standard Ligatures feature, may not be desired in all text settings.	ft → ft
HISTORICAL FORMS: This feature replaces the default (current) forms with the T historical alternates.	hist → hiſt
SMALL CAPITALS: Turns lowercase characters into Small Capitals. Forms related to Small Capitals, such as Oldstyle Figures, may be included.	Small → SMALL
ORDINALS: This feature replaces default alphabetic glyphs with the corresponding ordinal forms for use after figures.	1st 2a → 1st 2a
ALTERNATE FIGURES: This feature containing 11 sets is demonstrated in more detail on page 171.	1 → 11 1 1 1
STYLISTIC ALTERNATES: This feature replaces the default forms with stylistic alternates. Many fonts contain alternate glyph designs for a purely aesthetic effect; these don't always fit into a clear category like swash or historical. The features shown replace the default forms with stylistic alternates organized in one or more corresponding sets.	a → a J → J Z → Z 7 → 7 ÄÜÖ → ÄÜÖ

Typefaces used in Stop Stealing Sheep, 3rd ed.

23% serif	31% sans	11% script	30% display	5% symbols

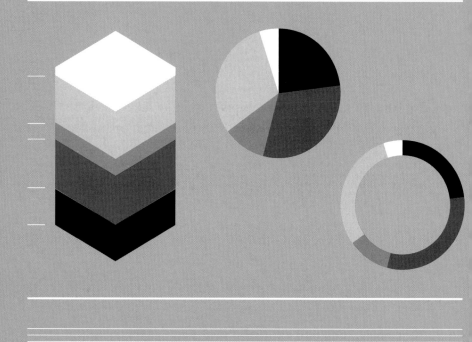

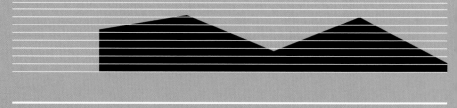

23+31+11+30+5

Fonts are a useful, space-saving, and simple way to access vector data from a keyboard. Charts and graphs represent data in vector form and are cumbersome to use and especially to correct once they have been generated as images.

Driven by the frustration of creating graphs within design applications, Travis Kochel took advantage of OpenType technology to simplify the process.

Primarily suitable for Adobe Creative Suite, FF Chartwell for print uses OpenType ligatures to transform strings of numbers automatically into charts. The data remains in a text box, allowing for easy updates and styling. You simply type a series of numbers like: "10+13+37+40." Turn on ligatures and a graph is created. Turn off ligatures to see the original data.

There is also a web version where all the chart drawing functions are provided as small JavaScript libraries. To create a chart you enter the values in a similar way to the desktop font and use HTML code to determine color and appearance.

This is how the print version is used:

1. Letter spacing set to "0" (zero)

2. The values 0–100 are typed, then "+" combines them into one chart. If the total is above 100, a new chart will begin. Using the letters *A–E* defines the grid for *Rose, Rings,* and *Radar. Bars Vertical* creates sparklines and other bar graphs, and *Lines* makes charts. *Layering* creates more complex diagrams.

3. Adjust the colors as you wish.

4. Turn on *Stylistic Alternates* or *Stylistic Set 1* and bingo!

To see the original data all you need to do is turn off *Stylistic Set* or *Stylistic Alternates.*

C+23+31+11+30+5

What if some members of your family can't sing? What if you need two sopranos, but only have one sister? Maybe you have three sisters and two brothers who can't sing or play an instrument. OK, then find yourself some outsiders, put them in the same sort of outfits, call them a "family"and everybody will believe you've been together all your lives. This is what Lawrence Welk did.

The typographic equivalent does not appear quite so harmonious. In fact, the idea is to bring in outside fonts that do things your basic family can't. Usually this means a few more heavy weights if you're setting text in a classic book typeface that hasn't got a bold, let alone an extrabold weight. Or you might need more contrast – magazine pages all set in one kind of type tend to look very gray. And then, some types look better in certain sizes, so this too has to be considered if you have text that has to be set much smaller or larger.

High-fashion designers call these things accessories, and typographic equivalents have to be chosen the same way: they have to fulfill a particular function while achieving an aesthetic balance with the main dress.

The best way to add typographic impact is to use extended typeface families such as Lucida, which include a sans serif and a serif; or a family such as ITC Stone, which has a sans serif, a serif, and an informal version.

Agfa Rotis, designed in 1989 by Otl Aicher, one of Germany's best-known designers, comes in four versions: Sans, Semisans, Semiserif, and Serif.

My ITC Officina was originally intended to be used for office correspondence; thus a sans and serif version to replace Letter Gothic or Courier.

A more daring way to add contrast and adventure to a typographic page is to invite members from other typeface families. It is generally all right to mix different types from the same designer (Eric Gill's Joanna and Gill Sans work well together, as do most of Adrian Frutiger's types), or from the same period, or even very different periods. There are almost as many recipes as there are fonts. The pages in this book are themselves examples of mixing different typefaces: Equity for text; and FF Unit, a sans serif in a bold weight at a smaller size (and in another color) for sidebars, and another weight for captions.

Handgloves
AGFA ROTIS SANS SERIF

Handgloves
AGFA ROTIS SEMISANS

Handgloves
AGFA ROTIS SEMISERIF

Handgloves
AGFA ROTIS SERIF

Handgloves
ITC OFFICINA BOOK

Handgloves
ITC OFFICINA ITALIC

Handgloves
ITC OFFICINA BOLD

Handgloves
ITC OFFICINA SERIF BOOK

Handgloves
ITC OFFICINA SERIF ITALIC

Handgloves
ITC OFFICINA SERIF BOLD

Handgloves
JOANNA REGULAR

Handgloves
JOANNA EXTRA BOLD

Handgloves
GILL SANS REGULAR

Handgloves
GILL SANS REGULAR ITALIC

Handgloves
GILL SANS BOLD

Handgloves
GILL SANS BOLD ITALIC

Now that we've begun the music/type comparison, let's use one more example from that world to illustrate another typographic feature.

There is loud music and quiet music, dulcet tones and heavy ones, and there is – did you ever doubt it? – a typographic parallel. Some typefaces are loud by design, some are rather fine and sweet. A good family of fonts will cater to all these moods.

To illustrate the widest possible range within one family, we've chosen a typeface of many weights and versions, Helvetica, beginning with the lightest weights to suggest the tones of a flute. Very light typefaces are for those messages we want to look delicate and elegant.

Helvetica is not the most elegant type design of all time, but it is practical and neutral, and it is seen everywhere. Designed by Max Miedinger in 1957, the family grew in leaps and bounds with different type foundries (Haas in Switzerland, Stempel and Linotype in Germany) adding weights as their customers created the demand for them. The result was a large family that didn't look very related.

When digital type became the production standard, Linotype decided to reissue the entire Helvetica family, this time coordinating all the versions to cover as many weights and widths as possible. To help distinguish among the 50 of them, they were given the same numbering system as the one originally devised by Adrian Frutiger for Univers (and since revised, as two digits were not enough to explain all the variants – see page 89); here the lightest weight is designated by a "2" in its name. The typeface has been renamed Neue (German for *new*) Helvetica.

gestalt
gestalt

Christian Schwartz redesigned not Neue Helvetica, but its mother, Haas Grotesk, and called it: yes, Neue Haas Grotesk. The top line is Neue Helvetica 95 Black, bottom is Neue Haas Grotesk 95 Black.

| 25 | 26 | 35 | 36 | 45 | 46 | 55 | 56 |

The flute makes light, delicate sounds; at the other end of the musical spectrum is the tuba with its undeniably substantial sound. As every music lover knows, a big instrument doesn't always need to be played at full volume, and a tuba will never work in the confines of a small chamber ensemble.

There are also limits to the use of very bold typefaces. At small sizes, the spaces inside bold letters start filling in, making most words illegible. So, like writing music for the tuba, the best thing for bold faces is to use them where you need to accentuate rhythm and lend emphasis to the other instruments and voices.

As letters get bolder, the white space inside them decreases, making them appear smaller than lighter counterparts. The type designer allows for this effect by slightly increasing the height of bolder letters. A similar thing occurs with the width of the letter – as the thickness of the stems increases, weight is added to the outsides of the letters, making the bolder weights wider than their lighter cousins.

By the time letters are very bold, they're usually called black or heavy, or even extra black or ultra black. There is no system for naming weights in a family, so for clear communication it is safer to use the number designations when talking about a large family like Neue Helvetica.

Once the weight of a letter has reached a certain critical mass and width, it begins to look extended, as well as extra bold. Extending a design adds white space to the counters (the space inside letters), so some extended black versions may appear lighter than their narrower black counterparts.

In the case of Neue Helvetica, there is one more weight beyond the 95 (black) version: 107, extra black condensed. If you look very closely you will notice, however, that the width of its stems is no greater than those of the black weight. Condensing letter shapes makes the internal spaces smaller and the type much darker.

Handgloves
65 NEUE HELVETICA MEDIUM

Handgloves
75 NEUE HELVETICA BOLD

Handgloves
85 NEUE HELVETICA HEAVY

Handgloves
95 NEUE HELVETICA BLACK

Handgloves
107 NEUE HELVETICA EXTRA BLACK COND.

HHHHHHHH

| 65 | 66 | 73 | 76 | 85 | 86 | 95 | 96 |

23 24 33 34 43 44 53 54 63 64 83 84

Rhythm and contrast keep coming up when discussing good music and good typographic design. They are concepts that also apply to spoken language, as anyone who has had to sit through a monotonous lecture will attest; the same tone, volume, and speed of speech will put even the most interested listener into dreamland. Every now and again the audience needs to be shaken, either by a change in voice or pitch, by a question being posed, or by the speaker talking very quietly and then suddenly shouting. An occasional joke also works, just as the use of a funny typeface can liven up a page.

There's only one thing worse than a badly told joke, and that is a joke told twice. Whatever typographic device you come up with, don't let it turn into a gimmick. A well-coordinated range of fonts will give you the scope for contrast as well as rhythm, and will keep you secure in the bosom of a well-behaved family.

Unlike Univers, Neue Helvetica does not have extremely condensed weights, but within the traditional family of Helveticas there are dozens of other versions, from Helvetica Inserat to compressed or even extra and ultra compressed weights.

Changing the typographic rhythm by the occasional use of a condensed or, indeed, extended typeface can work wonders. Remember, however, that space problems should never be solved by setting lengthy copy in a very condensed face.

Although large families such as Helvetica can make your typographic life easy, it won't be long before they become predictable; the proverb "Jack of all trades, master of none" comes to mind. One would be foolish to ignore the special fonts that have been developed to solve particular problems. If you want ultimate variety within one formal framework, just turn the page.

Handgloves

HELVETICA INSERAT

Handgloves

HELVETICA COMPRESSED

Handgloves

HELVETICA EXTRA COMPRESSED

Handgloves

HELVETICA ULTRA COMPRESSED

HHHHHHHHHHHHHHHHHHHH

37 38   47 48   57 58   67 68   77 78   87 88   97 98   107 108

You can have as many bands, groups, combos, quartets, and quintets as you like, but nothing surpasses a full orchestra when it comes to producing all the sounds a composer can dream up. Generally, orchestra musicians use instruments that have remained largely unchanged for several hundred years; however, nowadays the odd modern instrument might be included.

Again, all a little like typography. The instruments (our letters) have been around in very much the same shape for several hundred years, and the tunes (our language) haven't changed beyond recognition either. For classical page designs, we have traditional typefaces and our tried and true ways of arranging them on the page. Even new, experimental layouts work well with those types, just as modern composers can realize most of their works with a classical orchestra.

Today's type technology makes it easier to create closely related weights and widths than ever before. Provided you have good outlines and clean data, software can interpolate and even extrapolate almost infinite steps.

The Multiple master typefaces we featured in previous editions of this book have been superseded.

Multiple master typefaces were useful because they could be created "on the fly" by the designer or compositor when working in InDesign or other applications that supported the technology. Type design software now has that code built into it, so every type designer can use it to create those in-between weights and widths. That frees the user from making decisions and handling a technology that tended to be delicate, but it means that we are encouraged to buy not just the extremes of a family of faces and make up the members ourselves, but all of them.

Luckily, you can also buy single weights, even out of a large family like FF Clan. Buying a complete family, however, often offers a considerable discount. Beyond outright buying, we now have many new ways of using fonts, like subscribing to a service or renting them for a time or a project.

FF Clan is one of those incredibly useful type dynasties, made up of many families and styles. That versatility has led to the face being picked up by United Airlines for all its visual communication.

Near, far, and just about everywhere in between.
More than 370 destinations worldwide.

Ergonomics can be defined as the study of the dynamic interaction between people and their environments, or as the science that seeks to adapt working conditions to better suit the worker. People suffer if chairs are too low, tables too high, lights too dim, or if computer screens have too little contrast or emit too much radiation.

Children could tell stories about having to sit at adult tables, clutching forks that are far too big for them and having to drink from glasses they cannot get their little hands around.

This is similar to what has been done to many typefaces since the introduction of the pantograph in the late 1800s; the practice became even more prevalent with the advent of photo-typesetting in the mid-1960s. One size had to fit all. One master drawing was used to generate everything, from very small type to headline-size type and beyond. The multiple master optical size axis made it possible to bring out the variations in design details that allowed a type-face to be optimized for readability at different sizes. Twenty years later, that capability has been built into type design software.

Typographic ergonomics at last.

When type was made out of metal (see page 57), each size had to be designed differently and cut separately. The engraver knew from experience what had to be done to make each size highly readable. On very small type, hairlines were a little heavier so they would not only be easier to read, but also not break under pressure from the printing press.

When one master design is used to fit all sizes, as in phototypesetting and digital systems, these subtleties are lost, resulting in compromises that very often give type designs a bad name. This is especially true of the re-creations of classic faces: as originally designed, the types permitted only a limited range of sizes acceptable in terms of readability and aesthetics.

In 1991, Robert Slimbach designed Minion as a multiple master font. The technology made it possible to generate fonts that are optically adjusted for use at specific point sizes: the text sizes are clear and easy to read, and display sizes are refined and elegant.

Now that multiple masters are no longer supported, you can get these instances as normal weights in a font family called Minion Pro Opticals.

Handgloves
Caption

Handgloves
Regular

Compare the differences between the letter shapes and overall weight. The smaller design has heavier stems and serifs, wider characters, and a larger x-height.

Handgloves
Subhead

Handgloves
Display

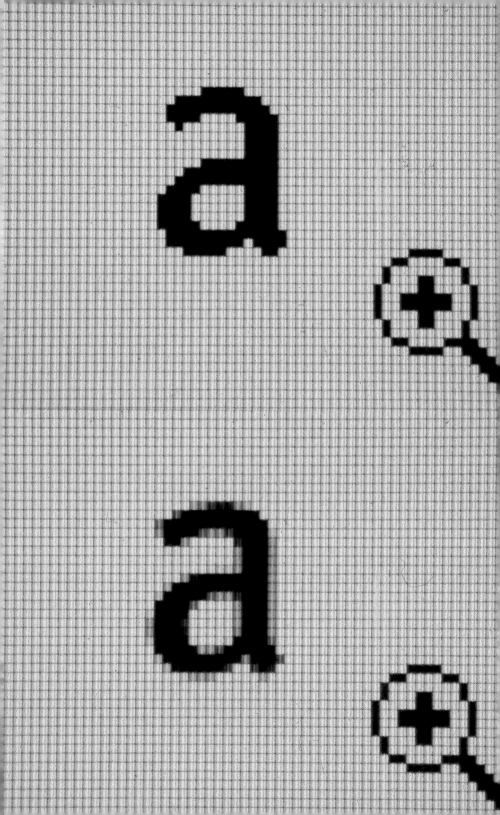

When this book first came out, computer screens looked and worked very much like TV sets. Flat screens were desirable but seemed unobtainable and too expensive. Flat LCD screens not only offer higher resolution, but the technology also allowed engineers to come up with more tricks to make bitmaps look acceptable to our eyes. Adobe developed *CoolType,* which uses color anti-aliasing. On old monitors, only whole pixels could be manipulated, but on digital LCD screens, *CoolType* controls the smaller red, green, and blue subpixels, individually adjusting their intensity. This effectively trebles the horizontal grid and achieves more precise smoothing along the edges of characters. A similar technology from Microsoft is called *ClearType.* Better screen resolution still doesn't mean that we can do without these manipulations to get type to look good on screen.

Our experience with the printed page shapes our expectations for other media. In order to make type on screens look acceptable to our physical requirements and cultural expectations, type designers now have to enlist the help of engineers and programmers. They fit unwieldy bitmaps into strict grids, then instruct the pixels to only appear in certain desired positions, and finally add gray pixels to the jagged outlines to make us see smooth curves where there are only coarse pixels. A lot of effort to overcome the inherent deficiencies of digital media.

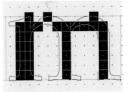

That's what happens when pixels try to fill outlines – some stems are wider than others and details like serifs disappear.

pack my box with
dog effect coffin ;
wyvern foxy syry
Of the greatest ar
look with too muc

pack my box wit
dog effect coffin
wyvern foxy syn
Of the greatest a
look with too mu

Hinting – the instruction of bitmaps to appear in regular, predetermined positions only – overcomes irregular letter shapes and random spacing. See page 177 to see what hinting does to the original outlines.

Our eyes can detect minute details that cannot even be measured. But science has become very good at exploiting some weaknesses in our perception. Three colors are enough to paint all possible rainbows, and shades of red, green, and blue make us see smooth curves.

typography

typography

Shades of gray make curves and diagonals appear smooth; this sample is enlarged from a small bitmap.

Anyone who would letterspace lower case would steal sheep.

Frederic Goudy
(1865–1947), American
typographer and
type designer, did not
design his first type-
face until he was forty-
five. He is noted for
his profusion of inno-
vative and eclectic
type designs and his
forthright declarations
on typographic issues.

CHAPTER 7

How it works.

FF Unit Rounded Regular

LETTERS WERE ORIGINALLY INVENTED to help communicate not high culture, but more mundane things like the amount of goods delivered or their value in barter or currency. What began as individual signs representing real items developed into letters and alphabets.

Different cultures added to the typographic variety. For instance, the most common vowel sound in an ancient language was also the the first letter of its alphabet. The Phoenicians (ca. 1000 b.c.) called it *aleph,* the Greeks (ca. 500 b.c.), *alpha,* the Romans (ca. 50 b.c.), *ah.* The Phoenicians had 22 letters in their alphabet; the Greeks added vowels, and the Romans developed the letters we still use today. All this time, people wrote either from right to left, or left to right, or top to bottom.

Tree farms are to forests what monospaced fonts are to real type.

With such a mixed history, no wonder our alphabet looks so unbalanced. Anyone inventing a new alphabet today would doubtless be more practical and make letters more regular. There would be more obvious differences between some shapes, and no narrow letters such as *l* in the same alphabet with wide ones such as *m.*

One consequence of our letters having such complex yet delicate shapes is that we have to respect their space. Every one of them needs enough room on both sides to avoid clashes with its neighbors. The smaller the type, the more space that's needed on the sides. Only big, robust headlines can support the occasional very closely spaced letters.

The history of type is a history of technical constraints. Mechanical typewriters gave us monospaced fonts. Each letter had the same amount of lateral space, regardless of its shape. Later developments led to typewriter fonts with more regular letter shapes; this did not necessarily improve legibility, but these newer alphabets no longer had any gaps between characters. They also appear extremely readable to computers, who don't care that much about tradition.

As soon as typewriters got little computers inside them, they were able to set justified text (lines of the same length), a style which was, and is, largely unnecessary in office communication. But people had learned from reading newspapers, magazines, and books that this was how type should be set.

Now technology allows us to typeset most of the alphabets ever created and actually improve on their appearance, definition, and arrangement. Proportionately spaced fonts are easier to read, occupy less space, allow for more expression, and are nicer to look at. There are only three reasons to still use monospaced fonts: to imitate the time-honored and personal look of typewriters, to write plain emails (see page 175), and to write code.

Himdgloves

Himdgloves

In monospaced typewriter typefaces, every letter occupies the same lateral space: the *i* is stretched on the rack, while the *m* suffers claustrophobia. The most common measurements are 12 characters to the inch (elite) or 10 to the inch (pica).

Letters, like trees, hardly ever appear by themselves. As soon as a bunch of letters are gathered together, they fight for space, for the right to be recognized, to be read. If you plant trees too close to each other, they'll struggle to get light and for space for their roots to expand; the weaker ones will stop growing and eventually die.

Before this turns into a tale of typographic Darwinism, let's look at the practical consequences as far as this book and its subject is concerned. If you know your text is going to be fairly long and that it will require some time to read, you should adjust the layout accordingly. The lines should be long enough to get complete thoughts into them and there ought to be enough space between them to allow readers to finish reading a line before their eye gets distracted by the next.

Marathon runners know they have 26 miles ahead of them, so it would be foolish to start off like crazy. There is also no need to run in narrow tracks, since by the time everybody gets settled into the race there will be plenty of room, with the first runners miles away from the last ones. With thousands of people in the race, individuals will blend into the crowd, but they still have to give their best.

Long texts need to be read the way a marathon is run. Everything has to be comfortable – once you've found your rhythm, nothing must disturb it again. If you have text that is going to require long-distance reading, design it so the reader has a chance to settle in. The rhythm depends on the spacing contingencies below.

Letters need to be far enough apart to be distinct from one another, but not so far that they separate into individual, unrelated signs. Mr. Goudy knew what he was talking about.

Word spaces have to be gauged so that the reader is able to see individual words, but can also group them together for quick comprehension.

The space between lines of type has to be generous enough to prevent the eye from slipping to the next line before it is finished gathering information in the current line of text.

The text below has been set for comfortable long-distance reading.

If time be of all things the most precious, wasting time must be the greatest prodigality; since lost time is never found again, and what we call time enough always proves little enough. Let us then be up and doing, and doing to a purpose, so by diligence we should do more with less perplexity. Sloth makes all things difficult, but industry all things easy. He that riseth late must trot all day and shall scarce overtake the business at night; while laziness travels so slowly that poverty soon overtakes him. Sloth, like rust, consumes faster than labor wears, while the used key is always bright. Do not squander time, for that's the stuff life is made of; how much more than is necessary do we spend in sleep, forgetting that the sleeping fox catches no poultry, and that there will be sleeping enough in the grave. So what signifies wishing

What did people do before there was the instant replay? A 100-yard dash is over in less than ten seconds these days, and spectators can't possibly look at each of the six or more contestants by the time they're across the line. Does that bring to mind the experience of thumbing through a magazine, with all those ads flashing by your eyes in split seconds? That's typography at its most intense. If you want to make an impression in an ad, you can't wait for readers to get settled in, and there is no space to spread your message out in front of their eyes. The sprinter has to hurl forward, staying in a narrow lane. In short-distance text, lines must be short and compact or the reader's eye will be drawn to the next line before reaching the end of its predecessor.

Setting text in short lines for quick scanning requires rearrangement of all the other parameters, too. Tracking can be tighter, and word spaces and line spaces smaller.

The choice of typefaces is, of course, another consideration. A type that invites you to read long copy has to be inconspicuous and self-effacing, confirming our acquired prejudices about what is readable. A quick look at a short piece of writing could be assisted by a typeface that has a little verve. It shouldn't be as elaborate as a display font used on a label or a poster, but it also doesn't need to be too modest.

If time be of all things the most precious, wasting time must be the greatest prodigality; since lost time is never found again, and what we call time enough always proves little enough. Let us then be up and doing, and doing to a purpose, so by diligence we should do more with less perplexity. Sloth makes all things difficult, but industry all things easy. He that riseth late must trot all day and shall scarce overtake the business at night; while laziness travels so slowly that poverty soon overtakes him. Sloth, like rust, consumes faster than labor wears, while the used key is always bright. Do not squander time, for that's the stuff life is made of; how much more than is necessary do we spend in sleep, forgetting that the sleeping fox catches no poultry, and that there will be sleeping enough in the grave. So what signifies wishing and hoping for better times? We may make these times better if we bestir ourselves. Industry need not wish, and he that lives upon hope will die fasting. There are no gains without pains. He that has

The above text has been tuned for sprint reading. Compare the long-distance text from the previous page.

While driving on freeways isn't quite as exhausting as running a marathon (mainly because you get to sit down in your car), it requires a similar mindset. The longer the journey, the more relaxed your driving style should be. You know you're going to be on the road for a while, and it's best not to get too nervous, but sit back, keep a safe distance from the car in front of you, and cruise.

Long-distance reading needs a relaxed attitude, too. There is nothing worse than having to get used to a different set of parameters every other line: compare it with the jarring effect of a fellow motorist who suddenly appears in front of you, having jumped a lane just to gain 20 yards. Words should also keep a safe, regular distance from each other, so that you can rely on the next one to appear when you're ready for it.

The tricky thing about space is that it is generally invisible and therefore easy to ignore. At night you can see only as far as the headlights of your car can shine. You determine your speed by the size of the visible space in front of you.

It used to be a rule of thumb for headline settings to leave a space between words that is just wide enough to fit in a lowercase *i*. For comfortable reading of long lines, the space between words should be much wider.

The default settings in most software vary these values, but the normal 100 percent word space seems just fine for lines of at least ten words (or just over fifty characters). Shorter lines always require tighter word space (more about that on the following page spread).

Theiwayitoiwealth

Ifitimeibeiofallithings theimostiprecious,iwasting timemustbeithegreatest prodigality;isinceilostitimeiis neverifoundiagain,iandiwhat weicallitimeienoughialways provesilittleienough.iLetius thenibeiupiandidoing,iand doingitoiaipurpose,isoibyidiligenceiweishouldidoimore

Ifitimeibeiofallithings theimostiprecious,iwasting timeimustibeithegreatest prodigality;isinceilostitimeiis neverifoundiagain,iandiwhat weicallitimeienoughialways provesilittleienough.iLetius thenibeiupiandidoing,iand doingitoiaipurpose,iso ibyidiligenceiweishouldido

A lowercase *i* makes a nice word space for headlines. Short lines should have modest space between the words.

You must have noticed that the lanes on the freeway are wider than those on city streets, even though cars of the same size use both types of road. This is because when traveling at high speeds, every movement of the steering wheel can cause a major deviation from the lane you're supposed to be driving in, posing a threat to other drivers.

This is, in typographic terms, not the space between words, but that between lines – the lanes that words "drive" in. Typographic details and refinement relate to everything else; if you increase your word spacing, you have to have more space between the lines as well.

One rule to remember about line space is that it needs to be larger than the space between words, otherwise your eye would be inclined to travel from the word on the first line directly to the word on the line below. When line space is correct, your eye will make the journey along one line before it continues on to the next.

The rest is simple: the more words per line, the more space needed between the lines. You can then increase the space ever so slightly between the letters (that is, *track* them) as the lines get longer.

If time be of all things the most precious, wasting time must be the greatest prodigality; since lost time is never found again, and what we call time enough always proves little enough. Let us then be up and doing, and doing to a purpose, so by diligence we should do more with less perplexity. Sloth makes all things difficult, but industry all things easy. He that riseth late must trot all day and shall scarce overtake the business at night; while laziness travels so slowly that poverty soon overtakes him. Sloth, like rust, consumes faster than labor wears, while the used key is always bright. Do not squander time, for that's the stuff life is made of; how much more than is necessary do we spend in sleep, forgetting that the sleeping fox catches no poultry, and that there will be sleeping enough in the grave. So what signifies wishing and hoping for better times? We may make these times better if we bestir ourselves. Industry need not wish, and he that lives upon hope will die fasting. There are no gains without pains. He that has a trade has an estate, and he that has a calling has an office of profit and honor. But then the trade

The miracle of computers has enabled line spaces to be adjusted in very small increments. In this example, none of the other parameters has changed – tracking and word space remain the same, but the line space increases. Notice how the more widely spaced lines cry out for looser tracking and wider word spaces.

In both driving and typography, the object is to get safely and quickly from A to B. What is safe at 60 miles an hour on a straight freeway with four lanes in good daylight would be suicide in city traffic. You have to adjust your driving to the road conditions, and you have to adjust typographic parameters to the conditions of the page and the purpose of the message.

Whether you're driving along looking at the scenery, or stuck in a traffic jam, or slowly moving from one set of lights to the next, you have to be conscious of the drivers around you. If they change their behavior, you have to react. When you learn the rules and have had a little practice, nothing will upset you, not in traffic and not in typography.

One of the best ways to keep the reader's attention on the content of your message is to keep the color of the printed text consistent. Newspapers do a very bad job of it. They agree that type, even in narrow columns, has to be justified. The result is words and lines that are erratically letter-spaced. Readers have become used to that style (or rather, lack of it); loose and tight lines of type, one after another, don't seem to upset anyone.

In other surroundings, however, lines that look a little lighter and then a little darker because no one has adjusted the spacing might make the reader think there is some purpose behind this arrangement: are the loose lines more important than the tight ones?

Again, and there is no guarantee this is the last time: every time you change one spacing parameter, you have to look closely at all the others and adjust them accordingly.

Longer lines need wider spaces: in these examples, line space, tracking, and word spaces have all been increased as the lines were widened.

If time be of all things the most precious, wasting time must be the greatest prodigality; since lost time is never found again, and what we call time enough always proves little enough. Let us then be up and doing, and doing to	If time be of all things the most precious, wasting time must be the greatest prodigality; since lost time is never found again, and what we call time enough always proves little enough. Let us then be up and doing, and doing to a purpose, so by diligence we should	If time be of all things the most precious, wasting time must be the greatest prodigality; since lost time is never found again, and what we call time enough always proves little enough. Let us then be up and doing, and doing to a purpose, so by diligence we should do more with less perplexity. Sloth makes all things

There are situations, and this really is the final car picture, in which normal rules don't apply. Space becomes a rare commodity indeed when thousands of people are trying to get to the same place at the same time. Some pages are just like a downtown traffic jam: too many messages, too many directions, and too much noise. One thing typography can do, however, that city planning cannot: we can make all of our vehicles different sizes, move them up and down, overlap them, put them into the background, or turn them sideways. A page like this looks better than your typical downtown gridlock.

S p a c

Traffic
Traffic
Traffic
Traffic
Traffic
Traffic
Traffic
Traffic
Traffic
Traffic

Overlap
Overlap
Overlap

Focus

Sideways

Perspective

Gridlock
Gridlock
Gridlock
Gridlock
Gridlock
Gridlock

Background
Background
Background
Background
Background
Background

If time be of all things the most precious, wasting time must be the greatest prodigality; since lost time is never found again, and what we call time enough always proves little enough. Let us then be up and doing, and doing to a purpose, so by diligence we should do more with less perplexity. Sloth makes all things difficult, but industry all things easy. He that riseth late must trot all day and shall scarce overtake the business at night; while laziness travels so slowly that poverty soon overtakes him. Sloth, like rust, consumes faster than labor wears, while the used key is always bright.

This copy is set to the same specifications as the second example on page 153, but reversed out.

If time be of all things the most precious, wasting time must be the greatest prodigality; since lost time is never found again, and what we call time enough always proves little enough. Let us then be up and doing, and doing to a purpose, so by diligence we should do more with less perplexity. Sloth makes all things difficult, but industry all things easy. He that riseth late must trot all day and shall scarce overtake the business at night; while laziness travels so slowly that poverty soon overtakes him. Sloth, like rust, consumes faster than labor wears, while the used key is always bright.

In reversed-out settings, the spaces between letters look smaller, because they are dark.This text is set with the letter-spacing (tracking) more open than in the example above.

If time be of all things the most precious, wasting time must be the greatest prodigality; since lost time is never found again, and what we call time enough always proves little enough. Let us then be up and doing, and doing to a purpose, so by diligence we should do more with less perplexity. Sloth makes all things difficult, but industry all things easy. He that riseth late must trot all day and shall scarce overtake the business at night; while laziness travels so slowly that poverty soon overtakes him. Sloth, like rust, consumes faster than labor wears, while the used key is always bright.

White type looks heavier than black type (dark color recedes, bright colors come forward), so we used a lighter optical weight of Minion.

If time be of all things the most precious, wasting time must be the greatest prodigality; since lost time is never found again, and what we call time enough always proves little enough. Let us then be up and doing, and doing to a purpose, so by diligence we should do more with less perplexity. Sloth makes all things difficult, but industry all things easy. He that riseth late must trot all day and shall scarce overtake the business at night; while laziness travels so slowly that poverty soon overtakes him. Sloth, like rust, consumes faster than labor wears, while the used key is always bright.

Often the problem is not that white type looks too heavy, but that the ink-spread from the printing process fills in the open spaces in and around letters. We have chosen a smaller optical size of Minion to make it a little sturdier.

1

If time be of all things the most precious, wasting time must be the greatest prodigality; since lost time is never found again, and what we call time enough always proves little enough. Let us then be up and doing, and doing to a purpose, so by diligence we should do more with less perplexity. Sloth makes all things difficult, but industry all things easy. He that riseth late must trot all day and shall scarce overtake the business at night; while laziness travels so slowly that poverty soon overtakes him. Sloth, like rust, consumes faster than labor wears, while the used key is always bright.

Remember: the more letters contained in a line, the more space that's needed between words and lines.

2

If time be of all things the most precious, wasting time must be the greatest prodigality; since lost time is never found again, and what we call time enough always proves little enough. Let us then be up and doing, and doing to a purpose, so by diligence we should do more with less perplexity. Sloth makes all things difficult, but industry all things easy. He that riseth late must trot all day and shall scarce overtake the business at night; while laziness travels so slowly that poverty soon overtakes him. Sloth, like rust, consumes faster than labor wears, while the used key is always bright.

For comparison among the various settings, the horizontal and vertical scales are broken down into millimeter units.

3

If time be of all things the most precious, wasting time must be the greatest prodigality; since lost time is never found again, and what we call time enough always proves little enough. Let us then be up and doing, and doing to a purpose, so by diligence we should do more with less perplexity. Sloth makes all things difficult, but industry all things easy. He that riseth late must trot all day and shall scarce overtake the business at night; while laziness travels so slowly that poverty soon overtakes him. Sloth, like rust, consumes faster than labor wears, while the used key is always bright.

4

If time be of all things the most precious, wasting time must be the greatest prodigality; since lost time is never found again, and what we call time enough always proves little enough. Let us then be up and doing, and doing to a purpose, so by diligence we should do more with less perplexity. Sloth makes all things difficult, but industry all things easy. He that riseth late must trot all day and shall scarce overtake the business at night; while laziness travels so slowly that poverty soon overtakes him. Sloth, like rust, consumes faster than labor wears, while the used key is always bright.

The first example has approximately 4 words (25 characters) per line and is set in 8-point type with 9-point line space (set 8 on 9); word spaces are very small and tracking is very loose. The second example accommodates 8 words (45 characters) per line, is set 8 on 8; word spaces are 10 percent wider and tracking is loose. The third block of text is set 8 on 11, with about 10 words (58 characters) to a line; the word space is opened another 10 percent, and the tracking is a little tighter. The fourth text block is set 8 on 12, and with 15 words (90 characters) per line, which is almost too wide. The word spaces are now at the default value, with a little tracking.

Symmetry is static – that is to say quiet; that is to say, inconspicuous.

William Addison Dwiggins (1880–1956) was a typographer, type designer, puppeteer, and author. The American book trade owes a debt to Dwiggins for bringing style and good design sense into mainstream publishing, most notably with the work he did on Borzoi Books for the publisher Alfred A. Knopf. He is responsible for reintroducing colophon pages, which give details about a book's typography and fascinating facts about the typefaces used. Caledonia, Metro, Elektra, and Eldorado are Dwiggins' typeface designs.

CHAPTER 8

Putting it to work.

FF Unit Medium

THE BED IS ONE piece of furniture that has escaped most design trends. Mattresses have changed and so has the technology of making bed frames, but the way we sleep is still the same and the basic bedroom looks just as it has for centuries.

Bedrooms and books have one thing in common: an essentially single purpose. Reading, like sleeping, hasn't changed much in several hundred years, although we now have reading glasses, and little lamps that clip right onto our books, and e-readers, like Amazon's Kindle.

It may be said that the forerunner of what we consider coffee table books existed in the early days of printing, showing small illustrations positioned in a narrow marginal column next to the main body of text. Paperbacks crammed full of poorly spaced type with narrow page margins are an unfortunate innovation but the intimate process of reading a book remains largely unchanged, as does the look of books.

Common to every book design is the underlying grid that divides the page into areas that serve different purposes – columns of text, marginal comments, headlines, footnotes, captions, illustrations. The more complex the structure of the text, the more possibilities for the arrangement of elements supported by this grid. Linear reading (as in a novel) usually just needs a straightforward, single-column layout, for which there are plenty of successful historical precedents.

The size of a book is crucial, but it is often determined by technical or marketing constraints. Books for serious reading should fit in our hands; it is preferable, then, to have a narrow format with wide margins that allow room for fingers to hold the book.

The column width (i.e., the length of a line of type) is governed by the width of the page, the size of type, and the number of words or characters per line. One or more of these variables is usually given, or is unavoidable, simplifying the other design decisions.

Type for extended reading should be no smaller than 9 point and no larger than 14 point. Point size is a fairly arbitrary measurement (see page 57), so these suggestions are valid only for "normal" book typefaces – types with a very pronounced or very small x-height need to be carefully evaluated.

The arrangements or layouts of our living-rooms still follow the same model they did generations ago. There is usually a comfortable chair or two, perhaps a sofa to accommodate more than one person, a table, a bookshelf, some lights. The only recent addition to this harmonious ensemble has been the television set, which took over the center of attention from the hearth.

Living rooms, as opposed to bedrooms, serve a multitude of functions. Families sit together, and when they're not all staring in the same direction watching TV, they might actually play games at the table, eat dinner (all staring in the same direction), or even pursue other interests such as reading, conversing, or staring in the same direction.

Certain types of books are used the same way: you can read, browse, look at pictures, or even check on something of particular interest. Pages offer various levels of entry for readers, viewers, and occasional browsers. These books will have to look different than our time-honored tomes of linear reading, just as living rooms look different than bedrooms.

Some books look like catalogs, some like magazines. Some have the structure of a typical novel, but with illustrations, either integrated into the text or on separate pages. The reader is likely to peruse this sort of book in a more casual fashion, so the designer needs to provide several levels of distinct typographic elements to act as guides through text and images.

If it has to be larger to accommodate pictures, or to provide room for text set in multiple columns, a book most likely will have to be set down on a table to be studied rather than read. This means that the margins can be smaller (no room needed for fingers to hold it) and that pictures can even extend to the edges of pages.

While books with only one level of copy usually need only one typeface in one size plus italic and small caps, more specialized books (such as this one) have to distinguish among the main text and other elements. This could mean a pronounced difference in type size; or perhaps another typeface with contrasting design or weight, or another color. In this book, we've employed a few of these devices at the same time.

If the contents, the illustrations, and the amount of copy vary from page to page, a flexible grid is needed. The one in this book allows for many different column widths, captions, and sidebars. These elements shouldn't be changed randomly on every other page, but when they do have to be adapted to varying contents, the underlying grid structure serves as a common denominator.

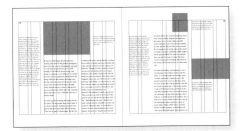

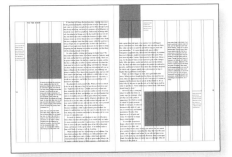

Hotel lobbies are institutional living rooms. Guests and visitors spend time there doing what they might do at home, but in the company of strangers. The dress has to be more formal and one's attention is more likely to be distracted by the things going on. There is still the opportunity, however, for all to sit staring in the same direction, watching TV. Some people manage to read real books in quasi-public places like hotel lobbies, but most spend their time there waiting for someone or something, so they are only able to read magazines. Magazine pages are designed for the casual reader: there are snippets of information or gossip (or one dressed up as the other), headlines, captions, and other graphical signposts pointing toward various tidbits of copy.

As advertisements change their look according to the latest cognitive fashion, editorial pages tend to either look trendier, or to deliberately stay sober, bookish, and authoritative.

Most magazines are printed in standard sizes; in the USA this means they're close to 8 1/2 by 11 inches. A line of type needs to be at least six words (between 35 and 40 characters) long, so the type ought to be about 10 point to arrive at a column width of 55 to 60 mm, or 2 1/4 to 2 3/8 inches. Three of these columns fit onto the page, leaving acceptable margins. The three-column grid is thus the basis for most publications printed on A4 = 210 x 297 mm. 8 1/2 x 11 inches = 216 x 279 mm.

To allow for other elements besides the main text columns, these measurements have to be divided again. Captions can be set in smaller type and in very short lines, so they might fit into half a basic column, making it a six-unit grid.

A good way to make these grids more flexible and spontaneous is to leave one wide margin that would only occasionally be filled with type. This grid would then have an odd number of units, say seven or even 13. The more complex the contents, the more supple the grid has to be, allowing for different stories in different-size types to occupy different widths.

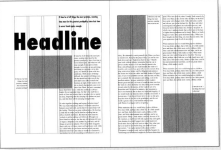

Kitchens are rooms with a clearly defined purpose: the storage, preparation, and often consumption of food and beverages. The equipment for these activities has changed considerably over the years and one could list numerous parallels to the development of typesetting systems over the same time span. The basic purpose has remained unchanged in both cases, whether it concerns food or type.

In a kitchen there are different surfaces for particular tasks, and containers and shelves for food, tools, dishes, pots, and pans. Graphic designers and typographers call the containers columns or picture boxes, the food is the text, the surface the page, and the tools are the typographic parameters needed to prepare an interesting page for the reader who has to digest it all.

Each recipe in a cookbook usually has explanatory text, a list of ingredients, and a step-by-step guide. It is sometimes illustrated either with small photographs or drawings. This sort of structure applies to any how-to publication, whether it's for car mechanics or landscapers.

People read cookbooks and other how-to manuals in situations that are often less than ideal. A cookbook has to compete for tabletop space with food, knives, towels, and bowls, and there is never enough time to read anything carefully. The text has to be read while standing, which means the type should be larger than usual. The recipe steps have to be clearly labeled with short headlines; ingredients and measurements should be in lists that can be referred to at a glance.

One of the best – or worst – examples of badly designed information is found in instructions for mounting snow chains onto the wheels of your car. This operation is usually done in the dark when you're wet, in a hurry, and uncomfortably cold. The instructions are often printed on white paper, which invariably gets wet and dirty before you've finished.

The typographic solution is to print them on the outside of the package, which should be made of some plastic material. The best color combination would be black type on a yellow background, which wouldn't show dirt as much as white. The type should be big and strong so it's legible no matter what. The text should be set in short, simple words and sentences.

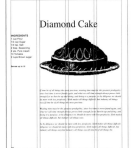

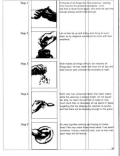

We spend much of our time outside our homes in places where our priorities are defined by other people. This is the case in most public places and, unfortunately, at work. Many people still have to work in conditions very much like this typing pool of the 1940s, even though it would be easy to improve the environment and thus the quality of work.

The same goes for much typographic work. There is no reason for hardworking pieces like price lists, technical catalogs, timetables, and similar heavy-duty information to look as ugly or complicated as they often do. If something looks dull, repetitive, and off-putting, people will approach it with a negative attitude (if they approach it at all). This does not improve their willingness to absorb the information.

Computers are a huge improvement over mechanical typewriters, and the output of laser printers certainly looks much better than anything that ever came out of a typewriter. To create good visual communication, however, takes much more than good tools. Whenever you come across those official-looking, unreadable pieces, don't blame it on the equipment.

Complex information, such as price lists and timetables, cannot be designed on a preconceived grid. The page arrangement has to stem from the content and structure of the information itself. First you have to find the shortest and the longest elements, and then ignore them; if your layout accommodates the extremes you will end up making allowances for a few isolated exceptions. The thing to do is to make the bulk of the matter fit, then go back to the exceptions and work with them one by one. If there are only a few long lines in an otherwise short listing, it should be considered an opportunity to flex your creative muscles: design around them or rewrite.

A sure way to improve the look and function of any information-intensive document is to eliminate boxes. Vertical lines are almost always unnecessary. Type creates its own vertical divisions along the left edges of columns as long as there is sufficient space between columns. A vertical line is wasteful because it needs precious space on either side. Use space to divide elements from each other. Utilize horizontal lines to accentuate areas of the page. The edge of the paper makes its own box and doesn't require more boxes inside it.

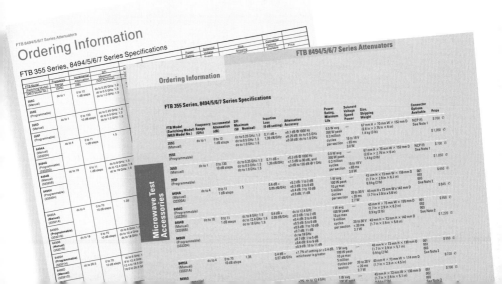

The typing pool is as old-fashioned as boxes on forms. Today's "information" workers still sit at a desk and type on keyboards, but they are allowed to move around, talk to other workers, get drinks, and actually exchange information with each other. Even the office cubicle, which was the successor to the typing pool, seems on its way out. And more liberal attitudes in our work space tend to show up in our design tastes.

Many menial tasks, such as typing the same information again and again, is done via the "copy and paste" command, and programs need just one keystroke to call up previously stored information about your address and credit card numbers. The biggest problem now is how to remember all your passwords without writing them down on a sticky note and displaying it on your computer screen for everyone to see.

A business that wants to attract good people and keep them motivated will have to indulge them a little. Talking to each other may be more important than counting key strokes. Relaxed work spaces, flexible hours, and flat hierarchies are all signs of a culture that judges people by their work and not by their strict compliance with corporate rules. If a firm still uses forms with lots of little boxes and redundant lines, it probably also keeps its employees in small cubicles.

Web pages will look very different on the user's desktop than they look on the designer's screen unless they conform to some widespread, and therefore sometimes bland, standards. Not every web page uses web fonts yet, so a lot of them still display Arial, Geneva, Verdana, and Times, certainly at text sizes. You can, however, define which fonts your browser will use to fill in the fields with your personal information.

For some very old and boring reasons, monitors driven by PCs use a different PPI (Pixels Per Inch) standard than Macs. So type on a PC won't look the same size as it will on a Mac. With today's high resolution screens, that doesn't matter very much anymore – it is just a small nuisance if you use different platforms for the same documents. Web designers code CSS (Cascading Style Sheets) to make sure that users see the same layout – if not at the exact same apparent size – in their browsers, irrespective of the platform.

If that is not the case, designers didn't do their job properly or you have a very old browser.

Identifier	Data	Description/Comments
First Name		
Last Name		
E-Mail a		
Tele		
Fax N		
Company		
Login		
Pas		
Pas		
Re-Identifi qu		

Billing Information

Please fill out the o order to complete yo informaton, you agre Limited ("Adobe") o such purpose.

Please enter your bil it appears on your c

First Name
erik

Company

Address
motzstrasse 58

City
berlin

Country of residenc
Germany

Email
erik@spiekermann.c

Use of Personal Information

☐ I would like to receive information and special promotions on Adobe products and services.

Adobe – Create an account
Adobe – Create an account

My Adobe account

Use your Adobe ID to download free trials, buy products, manage orders, and access online services such as Adobe® Creative Cloud™ and Acrobat.com. Plus, be a part of the thriving Adobe online community.

Create an Adobe ID
‹ I already have an Adobe ID

Adobe ID (Email Address)
jdoe@domain.com

Password

Retype Password

First Name

Last Name

Country/Region
United States

☐ Stay informed via email about Adobe products and services. Learn more.

1223	567
3445	564
6786	877
0034	651
2481	283
3274	000
2198	436
0004	765
7834	263
1223	567
3445	564
6786	007

48	6	3477	
8	578	347	6
56		5	73
6247	3	53	48
	9492		9
548	9765	2	7
6752	9	87	
358	9436	757	85
1678	6	76	
125	4	6	
723	5	1754	
6541	276	87	
	48	1	
65	71	7136	
8	6578	6	
87864	5		
76	58	7	
158		763	
565	5762	2	
6	74	3	
890		9	
1655	687	64	

76876	886	342342
56464	687	788787
24234	003	2344

7236	4437	98	75986
		753247	
652314	9823418	76872371	6675
2347653	4276542	3786	
876	2389734	278652	34
786523	78	5642	387
423874	2376542	3786	5
4237983	419	875	67812
65167257	69561		
234896	234876	423	87642
3874		878	234897
509	450	971	0913
490	72		
3487	6751	765234	7654
376542	376653	4587	64876
42317863	4287	2187	
6456458	74	58764587	23874
13876		4378	
901008	9364589	80	3413
483462	34675	324	
765231	4	9823418	
97	6872	37166	752347
34276			

MONTH					5	
SALARIES	8000				0000	10
FRINGE BENEFITS AND TAXES	2300				2300	
RENT	4600				1600	
INSURANC						
TRAVELIN	900	900	900	900	900	
FREIGHT	200	200	200	200	200	
REPAIR	100	100	100	100	100	
LEASING	0	0	2200	2200	2200	
TELEPHON						
OFFICE S						
JOURNALS						
LEGAL AN						
BANK CHA						
PHOTOCOP						
AUTOMOBI						
ADVERTIS						
CONSULTI						
OTHER						
SECURITY						
SUM						

Financial Statement
December 31, 2013

Assets			
Current Assets			
Cash	1,000		
Accounts Receivable	3,000		
Notes Receivable	1,500		
Merchandise Inventory		40,000	
Office Supplies			
Store Supplies			
Prepaid Insurance			
Total Current Assets		46,500	
Plant Assets			
Land	5,000		
Buildings		76,000	
Less Accumulated			
Depreciation	3,000	73,000	
Store Equipment		20,000	
Less Accumulated			
Depreciation	6,000	14,000	
Total Plant Assets		92,000	
Investments		50,000	
Patents		10,000	
Good Will	5,000		

Financial Statement			
December 31, 2005			
Assets			
Current Assets			
Cash		21,456	
Accounts Receivable	33,789		
Notes Receivable	31,012		
Merchandise Inventory	240,234		
Office Supplies		41,345	
Store Supplies	52,678		
Prepaid Insurance	323,567		
Current Assets	446,890		
Plant Assets			
Land		65,902	
Buildings			276,123
Less Accumulated		345,567	
Depreciation		73,234	273,456
Store Equipment			320,789
Less Accumulated	23,456		

Financial Statement			
December 31, 2005			
Assets			
Current Assets			
Cash		21,456	
Accounts Receivable	33,789		
Notes Receivable	31,012		
Merchandise Inventory	240,234		
Office Supplies		41,345	
Store Supplies	52,678		
Prepaid Insurance	323,567		
Current Assets	446,890		
Plant Assets			
Land		65,902	
Buildings			276,123
Less Accumulated		345,567	
Depreciation		73,234	273,456
Store Equipment			320,789
Less Accumulated	23,456		

Financial Statement			
December 31, 2005			
Assets			
Current Assets			
Cash		21,456	
Accounts Receivable	33,789		
Notes Receivable	31,012		
Merchandise Inventory	240,234		
Office Supplies		41,345	
Store Supplies	52,678		
Prepaid Insurance	323,567		
Current Assets	446,890		
Plant Assets			
Land		65,902	
Buildings			276,123
Less Accumulated		345,567	
Depreciation		73,234	273,456
Store Equipment			320,789
Less Accumulated	23,456		

Spreadsheets – as the name implies – need plenty of space. If you set them in Courier, you will end up with type that is small, and very easy to misread.

There are numerals that save space and that are still more legible than Helvetica or Times or those in your standard word-processor font. Figures in tables have to be the same width or they will not line up properly in columns. Lining figures (numerals that don't have ascenders and descenders) are usually tabular, and so do a reasonable job in this situation; lining figures are standard issue in most modern digital fonts.

For maximum legibility with added space economy, look at narrower-than-normal typefaces like News Gothic, at condensed faces like Univers 57, or at faces designed for this purpose, like Axel. These types will set your spreadsheets apart from the norm: not only will they look better, but they will also read better.

1234567890

1234567890

1234567890

1234567890

1234567890

1234567890

1234567890

1234567890

Our figures do not derive from the Romans, but from Indian mathematicians, and were then adopted in Persia and the Arab countries. That is why we now call them Arabic or Hindu numerals. We still use Roman numerals, but more for decorative purposes and mainly on movie posters and watch dials.

Numerals appear in different settings. In spreadsheets, they have to align underneath each other to form neat columns. They have to be easily distinguishable from each other and as large as space will permit. Within text, figures should be treated like words; they have descenders and ascenders like alphabetic characters and thus form an uneven outline like a word. That outline helps legibility (see page 107).

OpenType fonts allow for many features, which, in the case of figures, not only add aesthetic pleasure but also improve function. Tables are set in tabular figures (!): They all share the same width, as do other characters that are used in that context, for example, currency symbols and en dashes. Hyphens, commas, and decimal points should be a defined fraction of that figure space so tables line up vertically when all lines contain these characters as well as figures.

Identical twins look the same to everybody but their mother. Their differences are expressed more in their behavior than their looks. Distinct characters aren't always obvious at first glance.

OpenType features provide at least four different set of figures: tabular lining, tabular oldstyle, proportional oldstyle, proportional lining. There are also properly designed numerators and denominators to set fractions (as opposed to figures automatically reduced to fraction size or just the figures for quarter, half, and three quarters), specially designed figures for sub- and superscript, even figures to go with small caps, and there again lining or oldstyle. A slashed zero to distinguish that figure from an *O* or an *o* is also often present.

Proper Roman numerals should be set as small caps if within text, but not tracked as generously as a line of characters, because they are not, they just look like them.

MDMLXXXIV

MMXIV

1 proportional lining
2 proportional oldstyle
3 proportional small caps
4 tabular lining
5 tabular oldstyle
6 fractions numerators
7 fractions denominators
8 superiors
9 inferiors
10 bullets positive/negative

1 No 12345678900

2 No 1234567890

3 NO 1234567890

4 Nº 12345678900

5 Nº 12345678900

6 ½ ¾ ⅚ ⅞ ⁹⁄₉

7 ½ ¾ ⅚ ⅞ ⁹⁄₉

8 cm 1234567890

9 H_2O 34567890

10 ① ② ③ ④ ⑤ ⑥

Appearances are not false.

FF Bau

Paul Klee (1879–1940) was a German-Swiss painter whose work was imaginative, meditative, fantastic and playful. He gave his works ironic, irreverent, flippant and poetic titles.

Type
on screen.

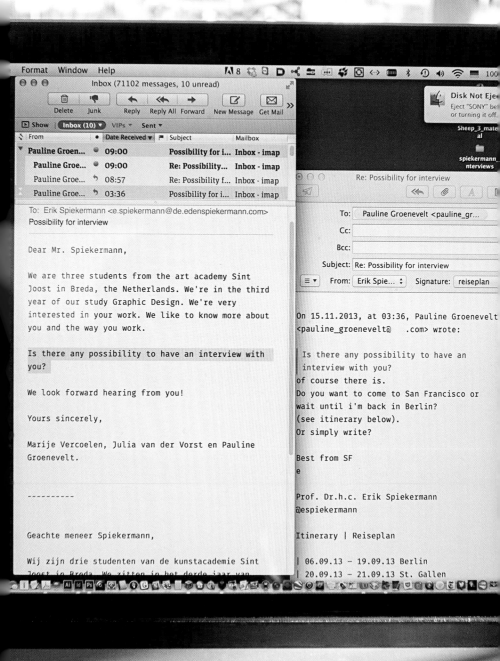

Disk Not Eje
Eject "SONY" bet
or turning it off.

Sheep_3_mate
al

spiekermann_
nterviews

Inbox (71102 messages, 10 unread)

Delete   Junk   Reply   Reply All   Forward   New Message   Get Mail   »

Show   Inbox (10) ▾   VIPs ▾   Sent ▾

From		Date Received ▾	⚑	Subject	Mailbox
Pauline Groen...	●	**09:00**		**Possibility for i...**	**Inbox - imap**
Pauline Groe...	●	**09:00**		**Re: Possibility...**	**Inbox - imap**
Pauline Groe...	↩	08:57		Re: Possibility f...	Inbox - imap
Pauline Groe...	↩	03:36		Possibility for i...	Inbox - imap

To: Erik Spiekermann <e.spiekermann@de.edenspiekermann.com>
Possibility for interview

Dear Mr. Spiekermann,

We are three students from the art academy Sint
Joost in Breda, the Netherlands. We're in the third
year of our study Graphic Design. We're very
interested in your work. We like to know more about
you and the way you work.

Is there any possibility to have an interview with
you?

We look forward hearing from you!

Yours sincerely,

Marije Vercoelen, Julia van der Vorst en Pauline
Groenevelt.

Geachte meneer Spiekermann,

Wij zijn drie studenten van de kunstacademie Sint
Joost in Breda. We zitten in het derde jaar van

To: Pauline Groenevelt <pauline_gr...

Cc:

Bcc:

Subject: Re: Possibility for interview

≡ ▾   From: Erik Spie... ▾   Signature: reiseplan

On 15.11.2013, at 03:36, Pauline Groenevelt
<pauline_groenevelt@   .com> wrote:

Is there any possibility to have an
interview with you?
of course there is.
Do you want to come to San Francisco or
wait until i'm back in Berlin?
(see itinerary below).
Or simply write?

Best from SF
e

Prof. Dr.h.c. Erik Spiekermann
@espiekermann

Itinerary | Reiseplan

| 06.09.13 - 19.09.13 Berlin
| 20.09.13 - 21.09.13 St. Gallen

Billions of emails are sent every day, more than letters, faxes and memos together. An email combines the advantage of a phone call with those of written communication: it is short and immediate, but provides proof of what has been said. Or so it should be. Netiquette, however, is not followed by everybody, which means that emails often turn out to be longer than phone calls and less legible than letters. The first thing to avoid is HTML formatting. This is the standard for text on the World Wide Web, but email programs that cannot read HTML will most likely display the message as unformatted text. This means that the text could run as wide as the window and have lines as long as 300 characters. Legible lines should be shorter than 75 characters, and many email applications automatically wrap lines at around that mark. Plain text messages contain no formatting in the first place, so you can be sure that it'll look the same to the recipient as it does to you. And because plain text can only be composed and read in monospaced fonts, the lines will break the same as in the original.

The second big issue concerns the reply button. Any phrase you highlight in your mail will automatically be repeated in your response. But even if you want to quote more than one contiguous sentence from someone else's email, you don't need to send it all back. Hit the reply button, then place your answer underneath the text you're referring to and delete all the other stuff. Or do your snail mail correspondents send your original letter back with their response? A little consideration for the recipient of your messages goes a long way.

Very simple email etiquette means that you don't burden all the recipients with constant repetition of old messages. Just highlight a relevant sentence and write your reply underneath it. This is email, after all, not literature.

For a bit of typographic choice, you could pick something other than Courier – for example Andale Mono. Even if the recipients don't have as much typographic taste as you do, the format you send will be almost exactly what they get.

Apart from consideration for the recipient and typographic vanity, we also need to be concerned with legibility of emails on our own screens.

At the recommended 12 point, differences between monospaced fonts can be quite explicit.

Handgloves 12
Handgloves 12

Even good old Courier exists in more than one version. Check your system fonts.

Handgloves 12
Handgloves 12

Andale Mono and Lucida Typewriter also come free with some programs.

Handgloves 12
Handgloves 12
Handgloves 12
Handgloves 12
Handgloves 12
Handgloves 12
Handgloves 12
Handgloves 12

If you want fine increments in weight, you have a look at Thesis Monospace. And there isn't even room to show the corresponding Italics ...

ATHIYAH, Kuwait —
y flows in via bank
is delivered in bags or
ging with cash. Work-
is sparely furnished
n here, Ghanim al-
ers the funds and
em to Syria for the
g President Bashar

— one of dozens of
o openly raise
the opposition —
n this tiny, oil-rich
tate into a virtual
outlet for Syria's
bulk of the funds

One Kuwait-based
money to equip 12,00
ers for $2,500 each.
paign, run by a
based in Syria ar
Qaeda, is called
With Your Mone
"silver status" b
50 sniper bullets
by giving twice
mortar rounds

"Once upon
ated with the
said Mr. Mt
in the Kuwa
American
out of Kuv

RTS C1-6

nging From Her Hea

ary Lambert found fame o
the hip-hop gay rights ar
e," but she seeks succe
tender music and poet

YORK A22-24

line Ambition

oning plan for th
d by Mayor Mic
en set aside.

Deal in G

ber of a pr
rs pleade
le feder

Car Mech.
Ease Birth

By DONALD G. M

An Argentine ca
method to retrie
bottle to develop
used to save a ba
canal.

It's Life Behir
Bulger

By KATHARINE Q. SEE
8:02 AM PST

Two life sentences plu
good measure mean B
notorious gangster wil
prison.

Judge Sides With
Scanning Suit

By JULIE BOSMAN and CLA
9:01 AM PST

A federal judge dismissed
Authors Guild, the latest ru
case seeking to stop the Goc
program.

Attacks Kill Dozens c
Officials Say

By THE ASSOCIATED PRESS

A suicide attacker and twin bor
Thursday targeted Shiites mark
religious ritual in Iraq, killing at
wounding more than 100 officials

Boeing Workers Reject
in Washington State

By NEIL

As content on the web continues to move from the desktop to the cell phone, tablet, and across social networks, web fonts can provide a consistent, branded experience no matter where a user encounters content. Publishers get instant brand recognition, while users benefit from an elegant, crafted typographic experience: a win for all.

For a few years now, web designers have no longer been reliant on the established system fonts such as Times and Arial, which are installed on all computers. Typographic emergency solutions using Flash or similar technology have pretty much become a thing of the past.

Web fonts are delivered in two formats: EOT (Embedded OpenType) and WOFF (Web Open Format Fonts). WOFF is a format specifically designed for web use with the @font-face declaration.

Web fonts are downloaded from a remote server and embedded using CSS and JavaScript. Fonts are "obfuscated" (packaged and hidden away), so they cannot be extracted and used for print. They require a special license. Companies like Typekit, Font Squirrel, Fontdeck, as well as the major foundries, provide this service and convert fonts to the appropriate formats. License models vary too widely to be quoted in a book. The same goes for specific technical details, which are bound to be redundant by the time the ink on these pages is dry.

Screens are not just new surfaces; they also require different layouts and ways to present content. Typography is the common denominator when moving a known brand across platforms. We recognize this newspaper even without the masthead.

A technical standard is all very well, but it does not guarantee that the same typeface will appear the same across browsers or platforms. The dreaded term "hinting" appears elsewhere in this book when we talk about presenting letters on screen or other modest-resolution surfaces. No amount of bending Bézier curves around to fit into grids, however, will ever accommodate every render engine on every system. Web designers will have to live with the fact that type will look different in different environments, just as it has done for centuries as papermaking, printing, and typesetting technologies changed.

The illustration below shows how far the outlines of Georgia have to change in order to fit the grid at different sizes. And this is one of the most thoroughly hinted screen fonts in the world! Automatically converting print fonts into web fonts will not get those results. For type used bigger than 14 or so pixels that won't matter so much, but it does for smaller sizes. That is why good old Georgia still dominates the web when it comes to reading long text.

In order for the bitmap on screen to look like the image on the right, the actual outlines have to be distorted as shown on the left. (Image courtesy of Petr van Blokland.)

Georgia 9px
Georgia 10px
Georgia 11px
Georgia 12px

H H

When Claude Garamond cut the punches for his typefaces back around 1530, he knew what the local printers in Paris needed. They printed with wooden presses on handmade paper and had to manually ink every page for each pull of the press. Type had to be as small as possible: More pages meant more work and more expensive paper. A small book fits in the reader's hand, can be carried around, and doesn't waste space on the shelf.

By the time Giambattista Bodoni cut his letters some 250 years later, presses were more sophisticated and paper was smoother. Printers could print finer lines and achieve better density on the page. Bodoni got away with the extreme contrast between thins and thicks that make his typefaces so beautiful even today.

Deep impression, ink smudges, and the paper itself had to be taken into account when designing a typeface for print.

Early screens were today's equivalent of handmade paper and the render engines were the wooden printing presses. Screen resolution is much better now, but type is still made up of pixels, and the look of fonts across different screens and browsers is anything but constant. So when you pick a typeface for text in small sizes that is meant to be read on a screen, remember Garamond. Don't sacrifice esthetics for practicality. Pick a typeface that has character and strength. Basically, the models which survived 500 years will look good on screens today.

Typefaces with reduced contrast, stronger serifs (or without serifs), and a reasonable weight are well suited for small screens. No serifs doesn't mean geometric: One of the earliest system fonts, Lucida, has good contrast and is very legible. That is why Apple even reworked it for its latest operating system.

Other system fonts have also been designed with the screen in mind but following traditional models. We read best what we read most. Microsoft's Segoe follows the humanistic model that makes Frutiger (the typeface) still one of the most useful and beautiful faces around.

Source Sans by Paul D. Hunt is a useful and good-looking typeface released under the Open Font License (OFL), which allows the licensed fonts to be used, studied, modified, and redistributed freely as long as they are not sold by themselves. Fira Sans and Fira Mono were designed for Firefox by Ralph Du Carrois and myself and also released under the OFL. These typefaces are available for free but that doesn't mean they're cheaply made. They were designed for screen but work equally well on paper.

FIRA SANS	LUCIDA	SOURCE SANS
Light	Regular	ExtraLight
LightItalic	Italic	ExtraLightItalic
Regular	**Bold**	Light
RegularItalic	**Italic**	LightItalic
Medium		Regular
MediumItalic	LUCIDA	RegularItalic
Bold	Regular	Semibold
BoldItalic	Italic	SemiboldItalic
	Demibold	Bold
FIRA SANS	Italic	BoldItalic
	LUCIDA SANS	Black
Regular	Regular	BlackItalic
Bold	Regular	
FIRA MONO	LUCIDA TYPEWRITER	SOURCE SANS

Handgloves
FF TISA

Handgloves
FF META SERIF

Handgloves
PROXIMA SANS

These three faces have been instant hits as webfonts, and for good reasons: they are sturdy but pleasant, useful but not overused.

Now that your wife has bought you a new suit, I don't mind starting up a correspondence.

Berthold Lo-Type Medium Italic

Groucho Marx
(1890–1977) was a
member of the Marx
Brothers, one of
the funniest comedy
teams in movie
history. In films like
Horse Feathers and
Duck Soup, Groucho is
perpetually punning
while displaying
a remarkable facility
for the leering look.

CHAPTER 10

There is no bad type.

FROM MEDITERRANEAN MERCHANTS making notes on clay tablets, to Roman masons chiseling letters into stone, to medieval monks moving quills across parchment – the look of letters has always been influenced by the tools used to make them. Two hundred years ago, copperplate engraving changed the look of typefaces, as did all subsequent technologies: the pantograph, Monotype and Linotype machines, phototypesetting, digital bitmaps, and outline fonts.

Most of these technologies are no longer viable, but some of the typefaces they engendered now represent particular categories of typefaces. Once again, the best example is the typewriter. As an office machine it is all but dead, but its typeface style survives as a typographic stereotype. Other recognizable typeface styles that have outlived their production methods are stenciled letters and constructed letters made with a square and compass.

Technical constraints no longer exist when it comes to the reproduction or re-creation of fonts from any and all periods. What used to be a necessity has become a look, just like prewashed jeans are supposed to make anybody look like a cowboy who's been out on the trail for a few months.

Designers have gotten good mileage out of the low-tech look. Theoretically, almost every typeface could be stenciled; all it takes is a few lines to connect the inside shapes to the outside so the letters won't fall apart when cut out of metal.

At almost the same time two designers had the clever idea of creating a stencil typeface. Stencil, designed by R. Hunter Middleton, was released in June of 1937; in July of that same year, Stencil, designed by Gerry Powell, was debuted.

Today anybody can make a typeface from any original. Rubber stamps, tea-chests, old typewriters, and rusty signs have been used as inspiration and often even as original artwork. Scanners and digital cameras bring it to the desktop. Then it takes skill, talent and serendipitous timing to turn an idea into a successful font.

Just van Rossum and Erik van Blokland were the first type designers to get all the ingredients right when they grabbed everything looking like letters in their attic and scanned it. FF Karton, FF Confidential, and FF Trixie don't hide their simple analog heritage while being perfectly functional digital fonts.

A true trend came out of Berkeley, California. Zuzana Licko of Emigre Graphics was inspired by the primitive bitmap fonts generated by the first Macintosh computers. She designed her own typefaces within those constraints. For technical reasons, some bitmaps are still there and these early designs show how stylish they could be.

Forty years ago someone at International Typeface Corporation realized that people wanted "honest" typewriter faces, but with all the benefits of "real" type. In 1974, Joel Kaden and Tony Stan designed ITC American Typewriter, which answers all those needs.

HANDGLOVES
STENCIL

HANDGLOVES
FF KARTON

HANDGLOVES
FF CONFIDENTIAL

Handgloves
FF STAMP GOTHIC

Handgloves
FF TRIXIE PRO LIGHT

Handgloves
EMIGRE TEN

Handgloves
OAKLAND EIGHT

Handgloves
EMPEROR TEN

Handgloves
ITC AMERICAN TYPEWRITER REGULAR

Handgloves
ITC AMERICAN TYPEWRITER BOLD

If a note is scribbled quickly, chances are the letter shapes in the words will be connected. Every stop, start, and pen lift of the writing hand slows down the process.

Neon signs and cursive fonts work hand in hand, so to speak. Neon tubes are filled with gas; the more interruptions there are in the continuous loop, the more expensive it is to make the sign. Signmakers therefore have to look for typefaces that connect as many letters as possible, or they must manipulate other types to accommodate the technical constraints.

The neon-sign style, in turn, influenced graphic design, and people have spent a lot of time airbrushing a glow of light around curved, tubular letters. Like other graphic manipulations, achieving neon effects has become much easier with drawing and painting programs available on the computer.

Signmakers working with neon take pride in their ability to select any old typeface and reproduce it with glass tubes. Because neon messages are generally short, the signmaker will most likely take the entire word and make it into one shape. Even if inspiration comes from available type styles, the glass literally has to be bent and shaped to fit the design and technical requirements.

Since most signs are original designs, there hasn't been much call for real neon typefaces, although some fonts with glowing shadows and curvy shapes exist on transfer lettering. Some typefaces look as though they could be useful for neon signs. They have strokes of identical thickness throughout and no sharp angles or swelling of curves. Kaufmann fulfills these criteria and possesses some of that 1930s elegance.

Handgloves

KAUFMANN

The warm glow of the tube is created with the help of Adobe Photoshop.

Handgloves

FB NEON STREAM

Handgloves

HOUSE-A-RAMA LEAGUE NIGHT

Handgloves

LAS VEGAS FABULOUS

Handgloves

FB STREAMLINE

Handgloves

FB MAGNETO

Welcome to the

PEMBURY
TAVERN

Cobra 0%
Beer
£2.50

TADDINGTON BREWERY
MORAVKA LAGER 4.4% £3

We associate particular typeface looks with certain products. Fresh produce always seems to want an improvised, handwritten sort of message, while high-tech applications demand a cool, technocratic look. Warm, cuddly products respond to a soft serif treatment, grainy whole foods are represented best by a handmade, rough-edged typeface, and serious money businesses always recall the era of copperplate engraving, when assets were embodied in elaborately printed certificates.

In some cases, this makes perfect sense. In produce and meat markets, where prices change constantly, time and expense prevent shopkeepers from having new signs printed each day. The most common solution is to write them out by hand; however, if the proprietor has illegible handwriting, it would be a disservice to customers to present an up-to-date but unreadable sign. The shopkeeper can simply buy a casual script or a brush font and print the signs reversed out on the laser printer. They will look almost like genuine handwriting on a blackboard.

Which one of these signs would you trust?

FRESH EGGS

Flying lessons

Fresh eggs

Flying lessons

Advertising, especially in newspapers, has always tried to emulate the spontaneous style of small-time shopkeepers and their signwriters. There were plenty of brushstroke typefaces available in hot metal days, even though the immediacy of brushstrokes and the rigidity of metal letters seem to be a contradiction. Many brushstroke typefaces now exist in digital form.

The names signal their potential applications: Brush Script and Reporter are the rough, brushstroke typefaces; Mistral, the most spontaneous design of them all, has already been praised in this book (see page 49).

With a little determination and a lot of software savvy, all of us today could make fonts. Some of these homemade fonts, sold by independent digital foundries, have recently become very popular. Among them are FF Erikrighthand, designed by Erik van Blokland, and FF Justlefthand by Just van Rossum, which began as practical jokes.

Handgloves
BRUSH SCRIPT

Handgloves
REPORTER

Handgloves
MISTRAL

Handgloves
FELT TIP WOMAN

Handgloves
FF PROVIDENCE

Handgloves
FF ERIKRIGHTHAND

Handgloves
FF JUSTLEFTHAND

Every language has its vernacular. It is considered the dialect of a specific group of people rather than a language of wider communication. The vernacular also has many vocabularies: the images we share, the music we attribute to a certain period, the TV series we remember – even the architecture that surrounds us.

Typography also has its vernacular. Not the traditional typefaces, designed for reading books or magazines, brochures, or newspapers, but rather the stuff local printers would use on a letterhead or shopkeepers for flyers in their windows. Movie titles used to be hand-made and designed according to the subject matter or the fashion of the time. We still recognize classic horror movies by their scraggy lettering, always with a dramatic drop shadow. We remember *Ben Hur* for the stacked title that looked like a colossal sculpture. Hanna Barbera, Disney, and all the other studios had their signature hand-lettered type.

Lettering originally meant that there wasn't any pre-made type, but artists sat down and designed each headline, title, and credit from scratch. When photosetting came about, lettering artists took their artwork and transferred it to strips of negatives through which one letter at a time was projected onto paper or film. The result was more mechanical than before because each character existed only in one version. So they added alternates, ligatures, and swashes to the character set, just like OpenType fonts have them today. The look of those titles, headlines, and slogans may appear quaint today, but they are still an inspiration for today's type designers.

The type on this wooden sign places it firmly in the American West of the 1800s, regardless of when it was actually made.

The computer was invented to take over repetitive tasks because it knows no boredom. Making computer-generated art appear spontaneous and lively is not easy. The same goes for type. Even variations can end up as mere repeats of similar patterns.

The House Industries guys in Delaware consider themselves lettering artists as well as type designers. They thrive on American vernacular. Turn to their library for typefaces, which look like they came straight from a beach bar in Hawaii or a 50s diner in Hollywood.

They took it upon themselves to digitize the entire Photolettering library, which had its heyday when advertising men ruled on Madison Avenue. The fonts manage to combine Flintstone aesthetics with digital finesse, a high-tech approach to portraying the low-tech culture that we'll always remember.

Handgloves
HOUSE-A-RAMA LEAGUE NIGHT

HANDGLOVES
HOUSE-A-RAMA KINGPIN

HANDGLOVES
HOUSE-A-RAMA STRIKE

HandGLOVeS
HOUSE MOVEMENTS CUSTOM

HANDGLOVES
HOUSE MOVEMENTS POSTER

Handgloves
HOUSE MOVEMENTS SIGN

Handgloves
HOUSE MOVEMENTS SOILED

HANDGLOVES
HOUSE MOVEMENTS

29.II 11 Goethes Tagebücher: Ein Mensch
Tagebuch hat, ist einem Tagebuch gegen
falschen Position. Wenn er z. B. in Go
liest 11.I 1797 den ganzen Tag zuhan
denen Anordnungen beschäftigt" so
er selbst hätte noch niemals an er
wenig gemacht. — Reise beobachtm
anders als die heutigen weil sie
Fortritsche gemacht mit den langsa
gen des Geländes sich einfacher ent
viel leichter selbst von demjenigen
werden können der die jene Gegend
Ein ruhiges förmlich landschaftliche
tritt ein da die Gegend unbeschädigt
eingeborenen Charakter dem Inzgaen
sich darbietet und auch die Land
Land viel natürlicher schneiden a
Eisenbahnstrecken zu denen sie viel
chen Verhältnisse stehn wie Flüsse zu Ka
braucht es auch beim Beschauer keine
keiten und er kann ohne große Müh
sehn. Augenblicksbeobachtungen g
wenige meist nur in Innenräumen wo
Menschen gleich grenzenlos einem vor d
ufbrausen z. B. österreichische Officiere in H
Stelle von den Männern

Typography is writing with mechanical letters. But as formal as our printing letters may have become, they still show traces of the hand. The rhythm of up- and-down strokes seems natural to our eyes, seriffed stroke endings betray the brush or the quill, and typographic terms like cursive remind us of the origin of our writing system.

Once we've mastered what schoolteachers still call "print," we move on to developing our own style of handwriting. This is often a compromise between personal expression and legibility for the sake of communication. Fountain pens and paper notebooks may be back in fashion, but more as fashion statements than actual writing tools.

The personal touch of "real" handwriting, however, is often used when a brand wants to convey a feeling of intimacy, of genuine one-to-one communication. Good idea, but difficult to turn into electronic form without a lot of scanning and reproduction work. Instead, we have typefaces that look like handwriting. A word-like letter with two identical e and l would show its mechanical origin if it weren't for OpenType features. Two or more versions of each letter can be designed and inserted automatically. Letter shapes at the beginning of a word are different from those at the end, some characters have alternate descenders or ascenders, and one can even have letters underscored or crossed out, as messy as your doctor's prescription.

Type designers have always been using their own handwriting as models for typefaces. Mechanical constraints and society conventions resulted in more or less formal scripts, executed with brushes, quills, fountain pens, and even felt tips. Those were then cut into metal or photographed and made into fonts. As digital tools became available and ever more sophisticated, handwriting fonts became more unconventional and personal.

You can now buy the "handwriting" of famous artists like Picasso, Cezanne, and even Franz Kafka. His manuscripts were rather messy, but that did not stop Julia Sysmälainen from designing her Mr. K with all the imperfections the writer would probably have liked to avoid.

An OpenType version of FF Trixie, the first digital "old" typewriter font, now uses features to make digital type look analog, while Suomi by Tomi Haaparanta looks like the handwriting you wish you had.

His handwriting, as digitized by Julia Sysmälainen.

The rigid typographic system of points and picas, of non-printing materials like reglets, furniture, quads and spaces, quoins, galleys and formes presented a challenge to those designers who wanted to make their work appear unconstrained, effortless, free-flowing even. It is ironic, therefore, that today – where the computer offers limitless choices to arbitrarily place elements anywhere on the surface, in any color, shape, or size – people should go back to letterpress printing.

There is one easy way out: Take the artwork from your computer and have someone make a polymer plate from it. That can be printed on a press, one color at a time, without the hassle of arranging the non-printing elements as carefully as those that will show up as inked messages. The tactile quality of printing into, rather than just onto, a surface will still be visible.

Arranging the space inbetween the letters is more work than setting the type itself.

If you want the full imperfections that come with the mix of materials – metal, wood, ink, paper – where each one adds to the list of things that can go wrong while trying to tame complex mechanical processes involving heavy machinery, electricity, chemicals, even compressed air, you can become a letterpress printer. Don't expect to make a living, but be prepared to learn your craft all over again.

Or you can simply fake it by using one of the many typefaces that have been revived from original woodtype. At least the visual effect will evoke the spirit, if not the body, of letterpress printing.

The trouble (or the fun) with letterpress printing is that you have to physically arrange not only the pieces that will eventually print, i.e. show on the page, but also the stuff in between: the non-printing space.

Large pieces, made from wood or metal, are called *furniture* and measured in picas. One pica equals 12 points and 6 picas equal one inch – at least that is the case within the Anglo-American typographic system.

Thinner pieces are called *reglet* or *leads*. They are used for the space between lines of type, thus the expression *leading. Quads* are used for spacing out a line of time and come in all sizes. An *em*-quad is a space that is one *M* wide, as wide as the height of the font. An *en*-quad is a space that is one *N* wide: half the width of an *em*-quad. Thinner adjustments are made with spaces, as thin as a sixth of the height. We still use these measurements in Indesign and other layout applications.

At the Hamilton Wood Type and Printing Museum, they still cut wood type. Here the router cuts a letter from Matthew Carter's Van Lanen, an exclusive design for HWT. Meanwhile, Richard Kegler of foundry P22 has been busy digitizing wood type from the collection.

HANDGLOVES
HWT VAN LANEN

HANDGLOVES
HWT AMERICAN SOLID

HANDGLOVES
HWT AMERICAN SHOPWORN

HANDGLOVES
HWT AMERICAN CHROMATIC

HANDGLOVES
HWT AMERICAN SOLID

HANDGLOVES
HWT AMERICAN OUTLINE & STARS

MANUFACTURED BY

Wm. H. Page & Co.

In ordering, leave out no part of the name or number printed over the line.

Twenty Line Chromatic French Clarendon Ornamented No. 4. Outside, Class E. 22 Cents. Inset, Class C. 15 Cents.

[Patented.]

SPOIL

Thirty Line Chromatic French Clarendon Ornamented No. 5. Outside, Class E. 32 Cents. Inset, Class C. 21 Cents.

DIN

Twelve Line Border No. 52. $1,25 per foot.

Printed with WADE'S INKS, from H. D. Wade & Co., 50 Ann St., New York.

No matter what turns technology takes, the typefaces we see most will still be those based upon letterforms from the end of the 15th century; the original Venetian or German models are evident in the diverse interpretations of every type designer since then. Garamond, Caslon, Baskerville, Bodoni; Gill, Zapf, Dwiggins, Frutiger: they all found inspiration in the past for typeface designs that were appropriate for their times and their tools. Every new imaging technology (as we call it today) results in a new generation of type designs. Today, outline fonts can emulate any shape imaginable, if not necessarily desirable; they can equal and even improve upon every aesthetic and technical refinement ever dreamed of or achieved.

When people today complain that there are too many typefaces around, show them some of the type specimens from the late 1800s. Those fonts were all manually cut, in wood or metal! They show that designing typefaces and making fonts have always fascinated artists, craftsmen, and designers, challenging them to make better and more beautiful things all the time.

Apart from the typefaces that work well because we are familiar with them, there are those that defy the simplistic classifications of usefulness or purpose. They may exist only because the type designer's first thought one morning was a new letter shape. These private artistic expressions may not appeal to a wide audience, but every now and again the right singer effortlessly transforms a simple song into a great hit. There are typographic gems hidden in today's specimen books just waiting to be discovered. In the right hands, technical constraints turn into celebrations of simplicity, and awkward alphabets are typographic heroes for a day.

There is no bad type.

It takes time for a typeface to progress from concept through production to distribution, and from there to the type user's awareness. Typefaces are indicators of our visual and thus, cultural climate; type designers, therefore, have to be good at anticipating future trends. No amount of marketing will get a typeface accepted if it runs against the spirit of the time.

Every once in a while a typeface is revived by graphic designers and typographers who dust it off and display it in new environments either as a reaction against prevailing preferences or simply because they want to try something different. Actual problem-solving often seems not to matter when it comes to choosing typefaces. True classic typefaces – that is, those with the beauty and proportion of their fifteenth-century ancestors, still win awards in the most chic and modern design annuals.

There is no bad type.

YOGI BERRA

WHEN YOU GET TO THE FORK IN THE ROAD, TAKE IT.

ITC Franklin Gothic Extra Condensed

Yogi Berra (*1925),
Hall-of-Fame catcher for
the New York Yankees,
was one of the great
all-time clutch hitters
and a notorious bad
ball hitter. Berra,
who later managed
the Yankees, has a
natural ability to turn
ordinary thoughts
into linguistic ringers.

CHAPTER 11

Final form.

Erik Spiekermann · Studentenfutter — Context

RHYME & REASON: A TYPOGRAPHIC NOVEL

Stop Stealing Sheep & find out how type works — Second

Stop Stealing Sheep & find out how type works

CARTER — A VIEW OF EARLY TYPOGRAPHY

TYPOGRAPHY FOR LAWYERS — MATTHEW BUTTERICK

JUST MY TYPE — SIMON GARFIELD

Kinross Modern typography — Hyphen

Kinross Unjustified texts — Hyphen

thinking with type A CRITICAL GUIDE — Ellen Lupton

Theodore Rosendorf — The Typographic Desk Reference

ParaType — Шпикерман О шрифте

Spiekermann über Schrift

FRED SMEIJERS — COUNTERPUN

KEITH HOUSTON — SHADY CHARACT&RS

THE FORM OF THE BOOK — Tschichold

Herbert Spencer Pioneers of modern typography

Paul Renner

Terwijl je leest — Gerard Unger

Band 1 Technische Grundlagen zur Satzherstellung

Band 2 Mathematische Grundlagen zur Satzherstellung

Niggli — Der typografische Raster The Typographic Grid — Hans Rudolf Bosshard

RONDTHALER — Life with Letters

TYPOGRAPHERS ON TYPE

Jost Hochuli, Robin Kinross Designing books

Documents on Typography

Jan Tschichold : Typographer   Ruari McLean

THE ENCYCLOPAEDIA OF Type Faces   BLANDFORD

gestalten   Ready to Print   📖 Handbook for Media Designers

Helveticaforever

LETTERPRESS   **The allure of the handmade**   David Jury

Carter Day Meggs   **Typographic Design: Form and Communication** Fifth Edition   WILEY

jan middendorp   dutch type   010   TYP.DU.001.00

THE CAMBRIDGE ENCYCLOPEDIA OF **LANGUAGE**   DAVID CRYSTAL   FA.TC.001.00   CAMBRIDGE

Hunt Roman   GENEALOGY

FontBook   FSI FontShop International   Digital Typeface Compendium   WWW.FONTSHOP.COM

Made with FontFont   BIS

American Wood Type: 1828-1900 / **Kelly**   TYP.AM.002.00   6500

Berry   LANGUAGE CULTURE T   TYP.LA.001.00   ATypI

ADRIAN FRUTIGER – TYPEFACES. **THE COMPLETE WORKS**   OSTERER STAMM   BIRKHÄUSER

Bibliography

Learning to use type properly might take a lifetime, but it will be a lifetime of fun. In case you have now been bitten by the typographic bug, here is what we recommend as further reading on the subject. The list is far from complete, but includes both practical manuals and classic works. Some of these books are out of print, but can be found with a little effort in good used book stores or online. Not that we suggest you do your reading online, but plenty of useful information about type and typography can be found on the web.

BERRY, JOHN D.
Language Culture Type: International Type Design in the Age of Unicode.
New York: Association Typographique Internationale, 2002.

BERRY, W. TURNER, A.F. JOHNSON, W.P. JASPERTS.
The Encyclopedia of Type Faces.
London: Blandford Press, 1962.

BIGELOW, CHARLES, PAUL HAYDEN DUENSING, LINNEA GENTRY.
Fine Print On Type: The Best of Fine Print on Type and Typography.
San Francisco: Fine Print/Bedford Arts, 1988.

BLUMENTHAL, JOSEPH.
The Printed Book in America.
Boston: David R. Godine, 1977.

BOSSHARD, HANS RUDOLF.
Technische Grundlagen der Satzherstellung.
Bern: Verlag des Bildungsverbandes Schweizerischer Typografen BST, 1980.

BOSSHARD, HANS RUDOLF.
Mathematische Grundlagen der Satzherstellung.
Bern: Verlag des Bildungsverbandes Schweizerischer Typografen BST, 1985.

BOSSHARD, HANS RUDOLF.
The typographic grid.
Zurich: Niggli, 2006.

BRANCZYK, ALEXANDER, JUTTA NACHTWEY, HEIKE NEHL, SIBYLLE SCHLAICH, JÜRGEN SIEBERT, EDS.
Emotional Digital: A Sourcebook of Contemporary Typographics.
New York & London: Thames and Hudson, 2001

BRINGHURST, ROBERT.
The Elements of Typographic Style. 2nd ed.
Point Roberts, WA: Hartley & Marks, 1997.

BURKE, CHRISTOPHER.
Paul Renner. The art of typography.
London: Hyphen Press, 1998.

BUTTERICK, MATTHEW.
Typography for lawyers: Essential tools for polished & persuasive documents.
Houston: Jones McClure Publishing, 2010.

CARTER, HARRY.
A view of early typography up to about 1600.
London: Hyphen Press , 2002.

CARTER, ROB, BEN DAY, PHILIP MEGGS.
Typographic Design: Form and Communication.
Hoboken, NJ: John Wiley & Sons, 2012.

CARTER, SEBASTIAN.
Twentieth Century Type Designers.
New York: W. W. Norton & Company, 1999.

CHAPPELL, WARREN, ROBERT BRINGHURST.
A Short History of the Printed Word.
Point Roberts, WA: Hartley & Marks, 2000.

The Chicago Manual of Style. 15th Edition.
Chicago: The University of Chicago Press, 2002.

COLES, STEPHEN (FOREWORD BY ERIK SPIEKERMANN).
The Anatomy of Type. New York: Harper Design, 2012; *The Geometry of Type.*
London: Thames & Hudson, 2013.

CRYSTAL, DAVID.
The Cambridge Encyclopedia of Language.
Cambridge: University Press, 1997.

DAIR, CARL.
Design with Type. Toronto and Buffalo: University of Toronto Press, 1982.

DONALDSON, TIMOTHY.
Shapes for Sound. New York: Matt Batty Publisher, 2008.

DOWDING, GEOFFREY.
Finer Points in the Spacing and Arrangement of Type.
Point Roberts, WA: Hartley & Marks, 1998.

DOWDING, GEOFFREY.
An Introduction to the History of Printing Types.
London: The British Library, 1997.

DRUCKER, JOHANNA.
The Alphabetic Labyrinth, the Letters in History and Imagination.
London: Thames and Hudson, 1997.

DWIGGINS, WILLIAM ADDISON.
Layout in Advertising.
New York: Harper and Brothers, 1948.

FRUTIGER, ADRIAN.
Type, Sign, Symbol. Zurich: ABC Verlag, 1980.
GARFIELD, SIMON.
Just my type: A book about fonts.
London: Profile Books, 2010.
GILL, ERIC.
An Essay on Typography.
Boston: David R. Godine, 1988.
GORDON, BOB.
Making Digital Type Look Good.
New York: Watson-Guptill, 2001.
GRAY, NICOLETE.
A History of Lettering: Creative Experiment and Letter Identity. Boston: David R. Godine, 1986.
HARLING, ROBERT.
The Letter Forms and Type Designs of Eric Gill.
Boston: David R. Godine, 1977.
Hart's Rules for Compositors and Readers.
London: Oxford University Press, 1967.
HLAVSA, OLDŘICH.
A Book of Type and Design. New York: Tudor
Publishing, 1960.
HOCHULI, JOST, ROBIN KINROSS.
Designing Books: Practive and Theory. London:
Hyphen Press, 1996.
HOUSTON, KEITH.
Shady characters: Ampersand, interrobangs and other typographical curiosities.
London: Particular Books, 2013.
JASPERT, W. PINCUS, W. TURNER BERRY,
A.F. JOHNSON.
The Encyclopedia of Type Faces.
New York: Blandford Press, 1986.
JOHNSTON, ALASTAIR.
Alphabets to Order: The Literature of Nineteenth-Century Typefounders' Specimens.
London: The British Library; New Castle, DE:
Oak Knoll, 2000.
JURY, DAVID.
Letterpress: The allure of the handmade.
Mies: RotoVision, 2011.
KELLY, ROB ROY.
American Wood Type 1828-1900: Notes on the Evolution of Decorated and Large Types.
New York: Van Nostrand Reinhold, 1977.
KINROSS, ROBIN ED.
Anthony Froshaug. Typography & Texts/ Documents of a Life.
London: Hyphen Press, 2000.
KINROSS, ROBIN.
Unjustified texts: Perspectives on typography.
London: Hyphen Press, 2002.

KINROSS, ROBIN.
Modern Typography: An Essay in Critical History.
London: Hyphen Press, 1992.
LAWSON, ALEXANDER.
Anatomy of a Typeface. Boston: D.R. Godine, 1990.
LAWSON, ALEXANDER.
Printing Types: An Introduction. Boston: Beacon
Press, 1971.
LEWIS, JOHN.
Anatomy of Printing: The Influence of Art and History on Its Design.
New York: Watson Guptill, 1970.
LUPTON, ELLEN.
Thinking with type: A critical guide for designers, writers, editors & students.
New York: Princeton Architectural Press, 2004.
MALSY, VICTOR, INDRA KUPFERSCHMID,
AXEL LANGER.
Helvetica forever: Geschichte einer Schrift.
Baden: Lars Müller Publishers, 2008.
MCGREW, MAC.
American Metal Typefaces of the Twentieth Century. New Castle, DE: Oak Knoll, 1993.
MCLEAN, RUARI.
Jan Tschichold: Typographer.
London: Lund Humphries Ltd., 1975.
MCLEAN, RUARI.
The Thames and Hudson Manual of Typography.
London/New York: Thames and Hudson, 1980.
MCLEAN, RUARI.
Typographers on Type: An illustrated anthology from William Morris to the present day.
London: Lund Humphries Publishers, 1995.
MCLEAN, RUARI.
How Typography Happens. London: The British
Library; New Castle, DE: Oak Knoll, 2000.
MEGGS, PHILIP B., ROY MCKELVEY, EDS.
Revival of the Fittest: Digital Versions of Classic Typefaces.
Cincinnati, Ohio: North Light Books, 2000.
MERRIMAN, FRANK. A.T.A.
Type Comparison Book.
New York: Advertising Typographers
Association of America, 1965.
MIDDENDORP, JAN.
Dutch Type. Rotterdamm: 010 Publishers, 2004.
MIDDENDORP, JAN, ERIK SPIEKERMANN, ED.
Made with FontFont: Type for independent minds.
Amsterdam: BIS Publishers, 2006
MORISON, STANLEY.
Type designs of the past and present.
London: The Fleuron, 1926.

MORISON, STANLEY.
First Principles of Typography.
New York: The Macmillan Company, 1936.

MORISON, STANLEY.
A Tally of Types. Boston: David R. Godine, 1999.

NICKEL, KRISTINA ED.
Ready to Print: Handbook for Media Designers.
Berlin: Gestalten, 2011.

OSTERER, HEIDRUN, PHILIPP STAMM ED.
Adrian Frutiger Typefaces: The Completed Works.
Basel, Boston, Berlin: Birkhäuser, 2009.

PIPES, ALAN.
Production for Graphic Designers. 3rd ed.
New York: The Overlook Press, 2001.

ROGERS, BRUCE.
Paragraphs on Printing.
New York: Dover Publications, 1979.

RONDTHALER, EDWARD.
Life with letters as they turned photogenic.
New York: Hastings House Publishers, 1981.

ROSENDORF, THEODORE.
The typographic desk reference.
New Castle, DE: Oak Knoll Press, 2009.

SMEIJERS, FRED.
*Counter punch: Making type in the
sixteenth century, designing typefaces now.*
London: Hyphen Press, 1996.

SPENCER, HERBERT:
Pioneers of modern typography.
London: Lund Humphries Publishers Ltd., 1990.

SPIEKERMANN, ERIK.
Rhyme & Reason: A Typographical Novel.
Berlin: Berthold, 1987.

TRACY, WALTER.
Letters of Credit: A View of Type Design.
London: Gordon Fraser, 1986.

TSCHICHOLD, JAN.
*Alphabets and Lettering: A Source Book of the Best
Letter Forms of Past and Present for Sign
Painters, Graphic Artists, Typographers, Printers,
Sculptors, Architects, and Schools of Art and
Design Ware.*
Hertfordshire, England: Omega Books, 1985.

TSCHICHOLD, JAN.
*The Form of the Book: Essays on the
Morality of Good Design.*
Point Roberts, WA: Hartley & Marks, 1997.

ULRICH, FERDINAND
(FOREWORD BY JACK W. STAUFFACHER).
Hunt Roman Genealogy. Berlin, 2012.

UNGER, GERARD.
Terwijl je leest. Amsterdam: De Buitenkant, 1997.

UPDIKE, DANIEL BERKELEY.
*Printing Types: Their History, Forms,
and Use. 2 vols.*
New Castle, Delaware: Oak Knoll, 2001.

WILLIAMSON, HUGH.
*Methods of Book Design: The Practice of an
Industrial Craft.* New Haven & London:
Yale University Press, 1985.

MAI-LINH THI TRUONG, JÜRGEN SIEBERT,
ERIK SPIEKERMANN.
FontBook. Digital Typeface Compendium. 4th ed.
Berlin: FSI FontShop International, 2006.

www.typophile.com
www.typographica.org
www.ourtype.com
www.letterror.com
www.typotheque.com
www.gerardunger.com
www.typography.com
www.fontsinuse.com
www.type-together.com
www.fontfont.com
www.fontfeed.com
www.houseindustries.com
www.commercialtypes.com
www.vllg.com
www.fonts.com
www.optimo.ch
www.adobe.com/products/type.html
www.linotype.com
www.itcfonts.com
www.fontshop.com
www.fontbureau.com
www.emigre.com
www.fontlab.com
www.typekit.com
www.wpdfd.com
www.hyphenpress.co.uk
www.quadibloc.com
www.ilovetypography.com
www.welovetypography.com
www.paulshawletterdesign.com
www.woodtyper.com
www.hamiltonwoodtype.com
www.typebase.com
www.kupferschrift.de
www.spiekermann.com/en
www.p98a.com
www.schriftdruckpapier.com
www.letteringandtype.com
www.urtd.net/projects/cod
www.typographyforlawyers.com
www.typerecord.com
www.typecache.com
www.typefacts.com
www.ffmark.com

Index

Typeface index

Credits

140
Marathon runners
Photo:
© Plainpicture,
Hamburg

142
Sprinters
Photo:
Julian Finney
© Getty Images,
Photonica World

144
Traffic jam in LA
Photo:
© iStock
by Getty Images

144
Freeway night
Photo:
© Plainpicture/ponton,
Hamburg

146
Traffic lanes
Photo:
© iStock
by Getty Images

148
City traffic
Photo:
© fStop

150
Cars on highway
Photo: Alex Maclean
© Getty Images,
The Image Bank

151
Noise
Photo:
Michael Balgavy,
Vienna

154
**William Addison
Dwiggins**

156
Bedroom
Photo:
Dennis Hearne,
San Francisco

158
Living room
Photo:
M. Helfer
© Superstock

160
Hotel lobby
Photo:
Dennis Hearne
(at Hotel Triton),
San Francisco

162
Kitchen
Photo:
M. Helfer
© Superstock

164
Typing pool
Photo:
© Historical Pictures/
Stock Montage

166
Edenspiekermann Berlin
Photo:
Edenspiekermann

170
Twins
Photo:
© iStock
by Getty Images

172
Paul Klee

174
Erik's e-mail
Photo:
Erik Spiekermann,
San Francisco

176
New York Times
Photo:
Erik Spiekermann,
San Francisco

178
H
Photo:
Erik Spiekermann,
San Francisco

180
Groucho Marx

182
Stencils and stamps
Photo:
Susanna Dulkinys,
Berlin

184
Neon sign
Photo:
Peter de Lory,
San Francisco

186
Chalk board type
Photo:
Ferdinand Ulrich,
London

188
Vernacular type
Photo:
Erik Spiekermann,
San Francisco

190
Kafka's handwriting
Franz Kafka,
Historisch-Kritische
Ausgabe sämtlicher
Handschriften, Drucke
und Typoskripte.
Hrsg. v. Roland Reuß
u. Peter Staengle,
Oxforder Quarthefte
1 & 2 (Stroemfeld
Verlag: Frankfurt am
Main, Basel 2001), I 92.

192
Letterpress at p98a
Photo:
Erik Spiekermann,
Berlin

194
**Specimens of Chromatic
Wood Type, Borders & C.**
Courtesy of
Nick Sherman

196
Yogi Berra

Erik Spiekermann (*30.5.1947) born 1947, studied History of
Art and English in Berlin. He is columnist (Blueprint, Form et al),
information architect, type designer (FF Meta, FF Meta Serif,
ITC Officina, FF Info, FF Unit, FF Unit Slab, LoType, Berliner
Grotesk and many corporate typefaces for The Economist,
Cisco, Bosch, Deutsche Bahn, Heidelberg Printing, Mozilla, etc)
and author of books and articles on type and typography.

He was founder (1979) of MetaDesign, Germany's largest
design firm with offices in Berlin, London and San Francisco. He
was responsible for corporate design programmes for Audi, Skoda,
Volkswagen, Springer Publishing, Heidelberg Printing, Bosch
and way-finding projects like Berlin Transit, Düsseldorf Airport and
many others. In 1988 he started FontShop, a company for production and distribution of electronic fonts.

He is board member of the German Design Council and
Past President of the ISTD International Society of Typographic
Designers, as well as the IIID International Institute for
Information Design.

In 2001 Erik left MetaDesign and now runs Edenspiekermann
with offices in Berlin, Amsterdam, London, Stuttgart and
San Francisco. In 2001 he redesigned The Economist magazine in
London. In 2003 he received the Gerrit Noordzij Award from
the Royal Academy in The Hague. His type system DB Type for
Deutsche Bahn was awarded the Federal German Design Prize
in gold for 2006. In May 2007 he was the first designer to be elected
into the Hall of Fame by the European Design Awards for
Communication Design.

In 2007, he was made an Honorary Royal Designer for Industry
by the RSA in Britain. In 2009, he became European Ambassador
for Innovation and Creativity by the European Union. The German
Design Council gave him their 2011 Lifetime Achievement Award,
the highest award in Germany. In May 2011 he was the 25th recipient
of the tdc Medal and also received the SOTA award. In 2012, the
Society of Typographic Artists in Chicago made Erik an Honorary
Member. In February 2013, the German Art Directors Club gave him
their Lifetime Achievement Award. Erik is Honorary Professor at
the University of the Arts in Bremen and has an honorary doctorship
from Pasadena Art Center.

Spiekermann lives and works in Berlin, London and San
Francisco. He owns 13 bicycles and has more than 300,000 followers
on Twitter.

Ferdinand Ulrich (*6.6.1987) is a Berlin-based typographer and type
historian. As a visiting scholar at Carnegie Mellon University in
Pittsburgh he began his research thesis on the typeface Hunt Roman
which earned him a graduate degree at Berlin University of the Arts
in 2012. As the assistant of Erik Spiekermann he has been setting
up an archive, helps on book projects and spends time experimenting
in the letterpress workshop P98a. He is also an adjunct lecturer
at Burg Giebichenstein University of Art and Design in Halle/Saale
(Germany).

Design
First edition: Erik Spiekermann, MetaDesign San Francisco
Second edition: Erik Spiekermann
Third edition: Erik Spiekermann & Ferdinand Ulrich

Typesetting, Layout, and Production
Erik Spiekermann & Ferdinand Ulrich

Picture Research
Susanna Dulkinys, Ferdinand Ulrich, Max Zerrahn

Primary text fonts are Equity and FF Unit.
Additional fonts were supplied by Adobe, FontShop International
(FontFont library), FontBureau, Emigre, House Industries,
Gerard Unger, P22, Commercial Type, Terminal Design, and
ITC International Typeface Corporation.

Matthew Butterick not only donated his typeface, Equity,
but he also indulged us by making some adjustments for the
typesetting of this book.

Sheep drawing courtesy of Chuck Anderson, csaimages.com